Gender Parity in Education and Employment Measured in 193 Nations.

Alan Bayham BA, MS

CHS, ASU, and UofP

Phoenix, Arizona USA

©2016

Abstract

Gender bias is an issue that faces all females in every nation throughout the world. Despite important advances in societies in relation to female rights, gender parity has not been reached worldwide, and the gender biases that persist throughout the world negatively impact females' rights to education and employment, which have disallowed them to achieve empowerment and equity similar to males within societies. Females have been historically discriminated toward in all countries in relation to education and employment opportunities, and these inequities are evident in both developed and developing countries today. There are, however, historical and contemporary gains that have been made toward equitable opportunities for females in most nations throughout the world, but gender gaps still exist in many nations throughout the world in relation to education and employment. In many nations, female education does not lead to improved employment opportunities, participation in the political process, and legal rights. The hypothesis that gender gaps have narrowed in relation to primary school completion rates, lower secondary school completion rates, upper secondary school completion rates, and employment to population ratios of 193 nations in the world was found to be true. Gender gaps, however, are still present in all nations today at many levels, especially in developing countries. This study shows that progress has been made toward gender parity throughout the world, but it has not been fully achieved yet.

Keywords: gender, bias, parity, male, female, employment, education

Gender Equality

The concept that life within societies should be based on equality and fairness is relatively new human history, and it is considered to be a characteristic of modern liberalism that emerged in the seventeenth century in Western Europe (Flax, 2007). Authors like Hobbes, Locke, and Rousseau are some of the most important liberal theorists from this period, and their writing reflected a new claim of equality rising in Western Europe during this period that rejected the natural basis of authority and feudal systems in place during this period. Public power in their view should be distributed equally and not on the basis of one's family origin or gender. These concepts laid the foundation for modern liberalism and the current social construct that most societies have today, which have resulted in greater freedom for the masses and the opportunity for participation in civic life for all citizens within nations.

Participation in the political process led to females advocating formal legal equality in most nations, and, by the twenty-first century, females had gained the right to vote, own property, work, receive education, and hold public office in the majority of countries throughout the world (Flax, 2007). Despite this progress, females are more likely than males throughout the world to be situated by race and class, and they are often subjected to the most dangerous work and make up the world's majority of illiterate inhabitants. Females, despite the progress made, still continue to be absent from public office, hold economic power, and undergo cultural subjugation in most societies throughout the world. Many feminists argue that the concept of gender is socially constructed to maintain male superiority and power within societies, and this social construct results in the suppression of females in areas of employment, family, politics, education, and sexuality. Due to females' reproductive capacity, they are disadvantaged biologically, which has not properly been addressed by the majority of societies throughout the world. This is a systemic disadvantage, and it has resulted in inequalities at multiple levels within societies throughout the world. These inequalities resulting in disadvantages based on sexual differences are seen as counterproductive to females, and, as a result of them, the majority of females in societies throughout the world are not equally situated to males as it pertains to reproduction, divisions of labor, and behavioral standards. Cultural norms within societies have caused socialization and identity formation that biases females' roles and individuals concepts of gender norms, which has resulted in females being permitted to conduct only domestic labor, childcare, and elderly care in most societies throughout the world. This has permeated all levels of societies, and it has had repercussions in public policies that favor males over females in social welfare programs, divorce law, and healthcare throughout the world.

The History of Females' Education

The adoption of movable type in Europe in the fifteenth century made education possible for this masses (Grendler, 2006). Prior to this period, education was only available for nobles and clergymen, and it was either delivered by the Protestant Church or the Catholic Church. The use of movable type made the reliance of scribes in the educational process obsolete, and scholarship became more widespread as the cost of printed materials declined. In the sixteenth century, a spread of literacy is attributed to inexpensive printed materials, free schooling, and the reward of scholarship in societies by nearly all historians.

As a result of people's increased desire to educate themselves and the social reward, scholars, like Martin Luther, began to promote the concept of universal and compulsory education for adolescents (Grendler, 2006). In Germany, the quality of education improved dramatically in the sixteenth century, which subsequently spread throughout the rest of Europe. The Protestant Reformation and Catholic Reformation resulted in the education of the noble class, clergymen, and some of the masses being educated by religious institutions in Europe and throughout the world for nearly two hundred years until the eighteenth century. Central governments during this period had no direct role in education, but this changed in the mid-eighteenth century when educational reform swept throughout Europe by those influenced by the Enlightenment concepts. This caused a separation between church and state, and the state became a direct force in the educational process within European societies. In Europe, during the Protestant Reformation and the Catholic Reformation, males and females were typically not educated together. Schools for females during this period were to prepare them for domestic work and to be well-mannered wives, and, in the Catholic Church, those who were educated in convents had the option to stay following their education to become nuns. Nuns were typically more educated than other females in societies during this period, and they generally became educators in charity schools throughout Europe for impoverished female children. This lasted in the Catholic Church until the nineteenth century, and the schools evolved to include education in both reading and writing during this period. Both the Protestant Church and the Catholic Church also offered catechism classes and Sunday school classes to educate youth in religious doctrine in which males and females were educated separately. Many clergymen during this period also supported themselves as educators away from the church, so, in reality, the church has continued to have an influence on education despite state involvement in the education of citizens since both the Protestant Reformation and the Catholic Reformation.

In the twentieth century, female education focused on basic reading and writing, and Western governments typically endorsed programs that prepared them for household economics (Baughman, 2007). Despite this being archaic by today's standards, this was actually beneficial to many young females who lived in rural areas because it allowed tax dollars to assist in funding basic education for them. The focus on home economics helped young females to gain practical training for being mothers and wives, which was directly a form of socialization that led to a lack of empowerment in societies. It, however, did increase the focus on child-welfare, and this subsequently led to increased rights for both children and females within societies. Most females did not attend college or university in the early part of the twentieth century, and the college and university systems available for females during this period were typically reserved for young females from upper-middle class families and wealthy families. Curricula focused on preparing these young females for leisurely traditions in all female institutions, which persisted throughout most Western societies until the second half of the twentieth century. During the twentieth century, it was normative to have male and female colleges, but a small number of females were permitted to professional departments at technical schools, colleges, and universities in Western countries, which slowly increased over-the-course of the century. The majority of these courses opened following World War I to females because of a societal need to have females in the roles of technical, legal, and medical professions. Females were typically discriminated against in the technical, legal, and medical workforce throughout the first half of the twentieth century, but the need for nurses and other professions increased during World War I and World War II, which resulted in an increased acceptance and domination of this field by females for nearly a century. The nursing profession gained increasing prestige during the first half of the twentieth century, and the profession became dominated by females following World War I. Females, during the first half of the twentieth century, were also permitted to teach in both primary and secondary institutions, but they were not typically able to work in administrative positions or to teach at the university level. Most females teaching at the university level were permitted only to teach in home economics and social work departments during the first half of the twentieth century.

Employment and Gender Equality

There has been significant progress in educating females and breaking down social barriers to assist them in entering the workforce throughout the world (The World Bank Group, 2014). There have been dramatic changes in the last 30 years in some nations, which have permitted females to gain education and enter the workforce. This has empowered billions of females throughout the world, but females still face a lack of basic freedoms and inequalities in regards to work opportunities in the twenty-first century in relation to their male counterparts. More than 50% of females globally have not been incorporated into workforces, and females still earn less than males and have fewer employment opportunities. Comparatively, more than 75% of males are employed, and they generally are able to acquire larger plots of land, work in more profitable sectors, and face less discrimination in most nations than females. In many countries, females are still legally discriminated against, and they are unable to inherit property, open bank accounts, and take out loans. This discrimination does not permit them to be empowered, so they can gain economic freedom and purchase the necessities to start businesses and become prosperous.

The gender gaps that exist in most nations are a result of public policies and cultural norms that result in the socialization of females that leads to a cycle of poverty, dependence on males, and lack of empowerment (The World Bank Group, 2014). Public policies must assist both males and females in gaining education and training that begins in their youth and continues throughout their lives to create opportunities in conjunction with empowering people at the individual level. These policies should incorporate national provisions that assist laborers and business owners to gain social protection through government programs that assist both sexes later in life and allow social protection for those in societies. Nations need leadership and innovative programs that increase efforts to end gender discrepancies in workforces and educational programs to empower all citizens, especially the more than 50% of females who are presently not empowered through employment in nations throughout the world. Empowering females through employment and policies that allow them the same access to education and business opportunities as males in societies has many benefits for all. These benefits include improved female self-esteem, less poverty, and increasing nations' gross domestic products. In regions over the last decade in which progress has been made, like Latin America and the Caribbean, they have seen directly measurable benefits from increased female employment. Regions throughout the world differ in areas in which specific improvement is needed, but the fact remains that individuals, regardless of gender, who are employed and have the opportunity to open businesses can better support their families and take a more active role in societies. The jobs that best empower females in societies differ from one nation to another, but, in general, it must be formal work that results in wages and benefits to gain the desired social outcomes. Females throughout the world engage in both formal and non-formal employment that is often not paid, specifically in Africa, Asia, and the Middle East, which results in social discrimination within these societies because it does not economically liberate them.

Gender equality within societies must be viewed from a multidimensional approach, and one of the key aspects of gaining this is sanctioning paid employment and benefits for females within nations (The World Bank Group, 2014). Most formal and non-formal labor is difficult to measure within nations throughout the world, especially if individuals are not employed full-time. Research has shown that full-time paid employment is a strong indicator of females' treatment within societies because it generally results in evidence that females are earning more money, getting benefits, and afforded opportunities within societies, similarly to their male counterparts. On nearly all economic measures throughout the world, females are more excluded than males, and the labor force participation throughout the world has not improved for females over the last two decades. Males are 200% to 300% more likely to have full-time jobs throughout the world, specifically in Africa, Asia, and the Middle East. Female participation in the workforce in Africa, Asia, and the Middle East is as low as 25% in some nations for females between the ages of 15 and 67. For females who are employed, they earn as much as 30% less for the same work as males in most nations throughout the world, which includes developed nations. Social norms throughout the world are a persistent problem as it pertains to gender equality, and females' work is seen in most cultures as undervalued in comparison to males' work. Nearly 50% of individuals polled in developing countries believe that males have more rights to employment when a domestic labor market has contracted. Females who are granted employment are typically disadvantaged within work environments as a result of socialization regarding gender norms within societies, which is typically reflected in their performance evaluations as well. Therefore, some progress has been made in assisting females to gain freedom through occupation, but there is still a lot more progress to be made to reach gender parity as it pertains to employment throughout the world.

Purpose, Rationale, and Hypothesis

The purpose of this study was to measure the level of gender parity in education and employment through an analysis of primary school completion, lower secondary school completion, upper secondary school completion, and employment to population ratios of 193 nations in the world with the exception of Nauru and the Vatican City State (Nations Online, 2016). The rationale of this study was to measure the impact of initiatives by government and non-governmental organizations in increasing female schooling opportunities and participation in labor markets throughout the world. There are more males and females attending primary and secondary schools worldwide than ever before, and there has been an increased acceptance of female education and employment, despite gender biases within cultures, throughout the world. Gender gaps in education and employment have existed throughout the world for centuries, and they still exist today. Primary and secondary school completion rates are measurable as well as annual employment to population ratios, so the impact of the narrowing of gender gaps as it pertains to education and employment can be statistically analyzed. The effect of increased female participation in schooling and employment, despite historical and contemporary gender gaps, is substantial in relation to empowerment and equality for females within society. The hypothesis of this study is that gender gaps have narrowed between the 1993 to 2003 time period and the 2004 and 2014 time period for 193 nations in the world with the exception of Nauru and the Vatican City State in relation to primary school completion rates, lower secondary school completion rates, upper secondary school completion rates, and employment to population ratios of 193 nations in the world with the exception of Nauru and the Vatican City State.

Methods

The first through the fourth measurements calculated the annual primary completion rate averages, percentage of change, and shift for females that were twenty-five years or older between the 1993 to 2003 time period and the 2004 and 2014 time period for 193 nations in the world with the exception of Nauru and the Vatican City State (Nations Online, 2016). The fifth through the eighth measurements calculated the annual primary completion rate averages, percentage of change, and shift for females that were twenty-five years or older between the 2007 to 2010 time period and the 2011 to 2014 time period for nations that reported annual primary completion rate data every year from 2007 to 2014 for 193 nations in the world with the exception of Nauru and the Vatican City State. The ninth through the twelfth measurements calculated the annual primary completion rate averages, percentage of change, and shift for males that were twenty-five years or older between the 1993 to 2003 time period and the 2004 and 2014 time period for 193 nations in the world with the exception of Nauru and the Vatican City State. The thirteenth through the sixteenth measurements calculated the annual primary completion rate averages, percentage of change, and shift for males that were twenty-five years or older between the 2007 to 2010 time period and the 2011 to 2014 time period for nations that reported annual primary completion rate data every year from 2007 to 2014 for 193 nations in the world with the exception of Nauru and the Vatican City State. The seventeenth through the twentieth measurements calculated the annual lower secondary completion rate averages, percentage of change, and shift for females that were twenty-five years or older between the 1993 to 2003 time period and the 2004 and 2014 time period for 193 nations in the world with the exception of Nauru and the Vatican City State. The twenty-first through the twenty-fourth measurements calculated the annual lower secondary completion rate averages, percentage of change, and shift for females that were twenty-five years or older between the 2009 to 2011 time period and the 2012 to 2014 time period for nations that reported annual lower secondary completion rate data every year from 2009 to 2014 for 193 nations in the world with the exception of Nauru and the Vatican City State. The twenty-fifth through the twenty-eighth measurements calculated the annual lower secondary completion rate averages, percentage of change, and shift for males that were twenty-five years or older between the 1993 to 2003 time period and the 2004 and 2014 time period for 193 nations in the world with the exception of Nauru and the Vatican City State. The twenty-ninth through the thirty-second measurements calculated the annual lower secondary completion rate averages, percentage of change, and shift for males that were twenty-five years or older between the 2009 to 2011 time period and the 2012 to 2014 time period for nations that reported annual lower secondary completion rate data every year from 2009 to 2014 for 193 nations in the world with the exception of Nauru and the Vatican City State. The thirty-third through the thirty-sixth measurements calculated the annual upper secondary completion rate averages, percentage of change, and shift for females that were twenty-five years or older between the 1993 to 2003 time period and the 2004 and 2014 time period for 193 nations in the world with the exception of Nauru and the Vatican City State. The thirty-seventh through fortieth measurements calculated the annual upper secondary completion rate averages, percentage of change, and shift for females that were twenty-five years or older between the 2009 to 2011 time period and the 2012 to 2014 time period for nations that reported annual upper secondary completion rate data every year from 2009 to 2014 for 193 nations in the world with the exception of Nauru and the Vatican City State. The forty-first through the forty-fourth measurements calculated the annual upper secondary completion rate averages, percentage of change, and shift for males that were twenty-five years or older between the 1993 to 2003 time period and the 2004 and 2014 time period for 193 nations in the world with the exception of Nauru and the Vatican City State. The forty-fifth through forty-eighth measurements calculated the annual upper secondary completion rate averages, percentage of change, and shift for males that were twenty-five years or older between the 2009 to 2011 time period and the 2012 to 2014 time period for nations that reported annual upper secondary completion rate data every year from 2009 to 2014 for 193 nations in the world with the exception of Nauru and the Vatican City State. The forty-ninth through the fifty-second measurements calculated the annual employment to population ratio averages, percentage of change, and shift for females who were fifteen years or older between the 1993 to 2003 time period and the 2004 and 2014 time period for 193 nations in the world with the exception of Nauru and the Vatican City State. The fifty-third through the fifty-sixth measurements calculated the annual employment to population ratio averages, percentage of change, and shift for males who were fifteen years or older between the 1993 to 2003 time period and the 2004 and 2014 time period for 193 nations in the world with the exception of Nauru and the Vatican City State.

Results

The first through the fourth measurements calculated the annual primary completion rate averages, percentage of change, and shift for females that were twenty-five years or older between the 1993 to 2003 time period and the 2004 and 2014 time period for 193 nations in the world with the exception of Nauru and the Vatican City State (Nations Online, 2016).

Country Name	1993-2003 Average	2004-2014 Average	% of Change	Female Primary Shift
Afghanistan	0	0	0	0
Albania	88.01961	92.92477	0.055728	4.905163
Algeria	0	46.82184	0	46.82184
Andorra	93.20574	94.48022	0.013674	1.274475
Angola	0	0	0	0
Antigua and Barbuda	0	0	0	0
Argentina	84.92394	0	0	-84.9239
Armenia	97.2563	99.22253	0.020217	1.96623
Australia	0	99.83546	0	99.83546
Austria	0	0	0	0
Azerbaijan	95.58738	97.34544	0.018392	1.758059
Bahamas, The	98.76429	95.27959	-0.03528	-3.4847
Bahrain	66.27708	63.87017	-0.03632	-2.40691
Bangladesh	41.50852	0	0	-41.5085
Barbados	86.39168	0	0	-86.3917
Belarus	0	98.62361	0	98.62361
Belgium	0	91.81472	0	91.81472
Belize	0	83.70303	0	83.70303
Benin	0	0	0	0
Bhutan	0	14.72378	0	14.72378
Bolivia	49.82854	45.90593	-0.07872	-3.92261
Bosnia and Herzegovina	0	66.02288	0	66.02288
Botswana	0	0	0	0
Brazil	0	74.53892	0	74.53892
Brunei Darussalam	0	0	0	0
Bulgaria	96.13315	0	0	-96.1332
Burkina Faso	0	4.997715	0	4.997715
Burundi	0	0	0	0
Cambodia	0	25.32679	0	25.32679
Cameroon	0	26.41038	0	26.41038

Canada	0	0	0	0
Cabo Verde	0	0	0	0
Central African Republic	0	0	0	0
Chad	0	3.47121	0	3.47121
Chile	0	84.00778	0	84.00778
China	0	0	0	0
Colombia	0	72.07103	0	72.07103
Congo, Dem. Rep.	0	41.36605	0	41.36605
Congo, Rep.	0	0	0	0
Costa Rica	0	79.26774	0	79.26774
Cote d'Ivoire	0	0	0	0
Croatia	88.06335	95.43849	0.083748	7.37514
Cuba	84.54508	90.31773	0.068279	5.77265
Curacao	0	0	0	0
Cyprus	0	90.24454	0	90.24454
Czech Republic	0	99.88493	0	99.88493
Denmark	100	100	0	0
Djibouti	0	0	0	0
Dominica	90.44652	0	0	-90.4465
Dominican Republic	0	63.58597	0	63.58597
Ecuador	0	74.79094	0	74.79094
Egypt, Arab Rep.	0	0	0	0
El Salvador	0	50.19321	0	50.19321
Equatorial Guinea	0	0	0	0
Eritrea	0	0	0	0
Estonia	99.12094	0	0	-99.1209
Ethiopia	0	14.8278	0	14.8278
Fiji	70.78718	82.77237	0.169313	11.98519
Finland	0	0	0	0
France	0	98.36823	0	98.36823
Gabon	0	0	0	0
Gambia, The	0	0	0	0
Georgia	97.7521	98.12222	0.003786	0.370115
Germany	0	99.99971	0	99.99971
Ghana	0	57.01071	0	57.01071
Greece	0	90.75549	0	90.75549
Grenada	0	0	0	0
Guatemala	27.6559	41.14379	0.487704	13.48789
Guinea	0	0	0	0
Guinea-Bissau	0	0	0	0

Guyana	67.85718	0	0	-67.8572
Haiti	0	0	0	0
Honduras	0	52.95323	0	52.95323
Hungary	98.23763	99.27907	0.010601	1.04144
Iceland	0	0	0	0
India	0	0	0	0
Indonesia	0	69.61459	0	69.61459
Iran, Islamic Rep.	0	0	0	0
Iraq	0	0	0	0
Ireland	0	0	0	0
Israel	0	87.6214	0	87.6214
Italy	89.88159	91.02859	0.012761	1.147001
Jamaica	0	99.35338	0	99.35338
Japan	0	99.83274	0	99.83274
Jordan	65.33705	77.34363	0.183764	12.00658
Kazakhstan	89.0745	99.99305	0.122578	10.91855
Kenya	0	49.14543	0	49.14543
Kiribati	0	0	0	0
Korea, Dem. People's Rep.	0	0	0	0
Korea, Rep.	86.41989	89.02052	0.030093	2.600638
Kosovo	0	0	0	0
Kuwait	0	58.09787	0	58.09787
Kyrgyz Republic	95.09947	97.26264	0.022746	2.16317
Lao PDR	0	0	0	0
Latvia	0	99.85266	0	99.85266
Lebanon	0	74.73006	0	74.73006
Lesotho	0	47.1239	0	47.1239
Liberia	0	0	0	0
Libya	0	0	0	0
Liechtenstein	0	0	0	0
Lithuania	0	97.90398	0	97.90398
Luxembourg	0	0	0	0
Macedonia, FYR	72.0068	0	0	-72.0068
Madagascar	0	0	0	0
Malawi	11.14737	0	0	-11.1474
Malaysia	79.96239	83.68854	0.046599	3.726147
Maldives	0	35.02406	0	35.02406
Mali	0	15.11645	0	15.11645
Malta	43.25044	97.19008	1.247147	53.93964
Marshall Islands	0	96.40101	0	96.40101
Mauritania	0	0	0	0

Mauritius	43.25044	63.34553	0.464622	20.09509
Mexico	62.24233	72.02052	0.157099	9.778194
Micronesia, Fed. Sts.	0	0	0	0
Moldova	0	98.55203	0	98.55203
Monaco	0	0	0	0
Mongolia	93.15181	95.57527	0.026016	2.42346
Montenegro	92.62019	95.97365	0.036207	3.35346
Morocco	0	0	0	0
Mozambique	0	16.87392	0	16.87392
Myanmar	0	0	0	0
Namibia	49.45998	0	0	-49.46
Nepal	0	0	0	0
Netherlands	0	98.25003	0	98.25003
New Zealand	0	0	0	0
Nicaragua	0	0	0	0
Niger	0	0	0	0
Nigeria	0	0	0	0
Norway	0	99.93001	0	99.93001
Oman	42.60187	57.68427	0.354031	15.0824
Pakistan	0	29.77113	0	29.77113
Palau	0	0	0	0
Panama	76.33286	82.4855	0.080603	6.15264
Papua New Guinea	0	0	0	0
Paraguay	64.24463	63.68284	-0.00874	-0.56179
Peru	0	70.59662	0	70.59662
Philippines	80.73994	84.23179	0.043248	3.491847
Poland	95.99619	98.15004	0.022437	2.153854
Portugal	73.30227	82.78416	0.129353	9.481885
Qatar	0	77.6868	0	77.6868
Romania	93.52966	97.64944	0.044048	4.119783
Russian Federation	99.67852	99.21157	-0.00468	-0.46695
Rwanda	0	26.80139	0	26.80139
Samoa	96.46191	99.12728	0.027631	2.66537
San Marino	0	0	0	0
Sao Tome and Principe	0	0	0	0
Saudi Arabia	43.77422	64.88093	0.482172	21.10671
Senegal	0	15.08089	0	15.08089
Serbia	68.67574	89.63997	0.305264	20.96423
Seychelles	94.27662	0	0	-94.2766
Sierra Leone	0	0	0	0
Singapore	0	78.28263	0	78.28263

Slovak Republic	99.60803	99.77772	0.001704	0.16969
Slovenia	0	99.28255	0	99.28255
Solomon Islands	0	0	0	0
Somalia	0	0	0	0
South Africa	65.34656	74.55576	0.140929	9.209206
South Sudan	0	9.58302	0	9.58302
Spain	0	85.53451	0	85.53451
Sri Lanka	83.4498	0	0	-83.4498
St. Kitts and Nevis	0	0	0	0
St. Lucia	0	0	0	0
St. Vincent and the Grenadines	0	0	0	0
Sudan	0	0	0	0
Suriname	0	86.04862	0	86.04862
Swaziland	0	0	0	0
Sweden	0	100	0	100
Switzerland	0	100	0	100
Syrian Arab Republic	33.44692	56.72643	0.696013	23.27951
Tajikistan	96.01507	0	0	-96.0151
Tanzania	41.7468	58.98379	0.412894	17.23699
Thailand	0	53.39789	0	53.39789
Timor-Leste	0	0	0	0
Togo	0	9.58302	0	9.58302
Tonga	100	96.09181	-0.03908	-3.90819
Trinidad and Tobago	0	93.00461	0	93.00461
Tunisia	0	0	0	0
Turkey	0	74.90127	0	74.90127
Turkmenistan	95.11101	0	0	-95.111
Tuvalu	0	0	0	0
Uganda	21.81093	9.58302	-0.56063	-12.2279
Ukraine	95.99108	0	0	-95.9911
United Arab Emirates	0	78.35872	0	78.35872
United Kingdom	0	99.76682	0	99.76682
United States	0	98.69626	0	98.69626
Uruguay	91.76545	86.83738	-0.0537	-4.92807
Uzbekistan	0	100	0	100
Vanuatu	0	0	0	0
Venezuela, RB	37.20672	80.69486	1.168825	43.48814
Vietnam	0	0	0	0
Yemen, Rep.	0	0	0	0
Zambia	0	0	0	0

Zimbabwe	9.58302	9.58302	0	0
	23.29514	**41.37992**	**0.776333**	**18.08478**

(The World Bank Group, 2016)

The fifth through the eighth measurements calculated the annual primary completion rate averages, percentage of change, and shift for females that were twenty-five years or older between the 2007 to 2010 time period and the 2011 to 2014 time period for nations that reported annual primary completion rate data every year from 2007 to 2014 for 193 nations in the world with the exception of Nauru and the Vatican City State (Nations Online, 2016).

Country Name	2007-2010 Average	2011-2014 Average	% of Change	Female Primary Shift
Azerbaijan	96.86	97.83	0.01	0.96
Cyprus	89.93	92.31	0.03	2.38
Czech Republic	99.88	99.89	0.00	0.01
France	98.81	97.92	-0.01	-0.90
Germany	100.00	100.00	0.00	0.00
Latvia	99.86	99.94	0.00	0.08
Lithuania	97.65	98.33	0.01	0.68
Moldova	98.28	98.83	0.01	0.55
Netherlands	98.31	98.24	0.00	-0.07
Peru	67.36	74.09	0.10	6.72
Portugal	82.86	85.25	0.03	2.39
Qatar	77.22	81.54	0.06	4.32
Romania	97.23	98.07	0.01	0.84
Singapore	76.33	81.35	0.07	5.02
Slovenia	98.82	99.66	0.01	0.84
Turkey	73.75	80.55	0.09	6.80
	90.82	**92.74**	**0.02**	**1.91**

(The World Bank Group, 2016)

The ninth through the twelfth measurements calculated the annual primary completion rate averages, percentage of change, and shift for males that were twenty-five years or older between the 1993 to 2003 time period and the 2004 and 2014 time period for 193 nations in the world with the exception of Nauru and the Vatican City State (Nations Online, 2016).

Country Name	1993-2003 Average	2004-2014 Average	% of Change	Male Primary Shift
Afghanistan	0	0	0	0
Albania	94.84628	96.38988	0.016275	1.543603
Algeria	0	64.06569	0	64.06569
Andorra	95.66563	96.05707	0.004092	0.391438
Angola	0	0	0	0
Antigua and Barbuda	0	0	0	0
Argentina	85.95408	0	0	-85.9541
Armenia	98.65564	99.52137	0.008775	0.86573
Australia	0	99.93626	0	99.93626
Austria	0	0	0	0
Azerbaijan	98.56658	98.99891	0.004386	0.432325
Bahamas, The	98.15744	94.85048	-0.03369	-3.30696
Bahrain	88.15903	70.46686	-0.20068	-17.6922
Bangladesh	52.86265	0	0	-52.8627
Barbados	86.35166	0	0	-86.3517
Belarus	0	99.55136	0	99.55136
Belgium	0	94.20308	0	94.20308
Belize	0	84.43343	0	84.43343
Benin	0	0	0	0
Bhutan	0	26.32747	0	26.32747
Bolivia	66.78459	57.38764	-0.14071	-9.39695
Bosnia and Herzegovina	0	85.11932	0	85.11932
Botswana	0	0	0	0
Brazil	0	73.49803	0	73.49803
Brunei Darussalam	0	0	0	0
Bulgaria	97.93366	0	0	-97.9337
Burkina Faso	0	11.92598	0	11.92598
Burundi	0	0	0	0
Cambodia	0	47.72083	0	47.72083
Cameroon	0	46.9952	0	46.9952
Canada	0	0	0	0
Cabo Verde	0	0	0	0
Central African Republic	0	0	0	0
Chad	0	14.29244	0	14.29244
Chile	0	85.6735	0	85.6735
China	0	0	0	0
Colombia	0	71.45024	0	71.45024
Congo, Dem. Rep.	0	74.02975	0	74.02975
Congo, Rep.	0	0	0	0
Costa Rica	0	80.13177	0	80.13177
Cote d'Ivoire	0	0	0	0
Croatia	95.42607	98.69674	0.034274	3.27067

Cuba	87.36432	92.10223	0.054232	4.73791
Curacao	0	0	0	0
Cyprus	0	95.62568	0	95.62568
Czech Republic	0	99.84898	0	99.84898
Denmark	100	100	0	0
Djibouti	0	0	0	0
Dominica	88.42652	0	0	-88.4265
Dominican Republic	0	62.54298	0	62.54298
Ecuador	0	77.94248	0	77.94248
Egypt, Arab Rep.	0	0	0	0
El Salvador	0	57.92757	0	57.92757
Equatorial Guinea	0	0	0	0
Eritrea	0	0	0	0
Estonia	99.48246	0	0	-99.4825
Ethiopia	0	36.50009	0	36.50009
Fiji	75.75222	82.81606	0.093249	7.06384
Finland	0	0	0	0
France	0	98.65477	0	98.65477
Gabon	0	0	0	0
Gambia, The	0	0	0	0
Georgia	98.89705	98.85306	-0.00044	-0.044
Germany	0	100	0	100
Ghana	0	73.35805	0	73.35805
Greece	0	95.20261	0	95.20261
Grenada	0	0	0	0
Guatemala	35.30976	49.24931	0.394779	13.93955
Guinea	0	0	0	0
Guinea-Bissau	0	0	0	0
Guyana	67.12315	0	0	-67.1232
Haiti	0	0	0	0
Honduras	0	52.05235	0	52.05235
Hungary	98.71617	99.4973	0.007913	0.781127
Iceland	0	0	0	0
India	0	0	0	0
Indonesia	0	79.30356	0	79.30356
Iran, Islamic Rep.	0	0	0	0
Iraq	0	0	0	0
Ireland	0	0	0	0
Israel	0	96.12005	0	96.12005
Italy	94.4656	95.71227	0.013197	1.246666
Jamaica	0	99.13703	0	99.13703
Japan	0	99.89135	0	99.89135
Jordan	71.80366	88.17261	0.227968	16.36895

Kazakhstan	92.8108	99.97245	0.077164	7.16165
Kenya	0	59.00504	0	59.00504
Kiribati	0	0	0	0
Korea, Dem. People's Rep.	0	0	0	0
Korea, Rep.	95.7592	96.9123	0.012042	1.153105
Kosovo	0	0	0	0
Kuwait	0	54.38509	0	54.38509
Kyrgyz Republic	98.07091	98.72121	0.006631	0.6503
Lao PDR	0	0	0	0
Latvia	0	99.87418	0	99.87418
Lebanon	0	82.52507	0	82.52507
Lesotho	0	34.03131	0	34.03131
Liberia	0	0	0	0
Libya	0	0	0	0
Liechtenstein	0	0	0	0
Lithuania	0	98.87061	0	98.87061
Luxembourg	0	0	0	0
Macedonia, FYR	85.33916	0	0	-85.3392
Madagascar	0	0	0	0
Malawi	28.75968	0	0	-28.7597
Malaysia	89.51134	92.29317	0.031078	2.781833
Maldives	0	42.87336	0	42.87336
Mali	0	20.50484	0	20.50484
Malta	55.35171	98.22859	0.774626	42.87688
Marshall Islands	0	96.45839	0	96.45839
Mauritania	0	0	0	0
Mauritius	55.35171	70.83129	0.279659	15.47958
Mexico	67.20482	75.58907	0.124757	8.384253
Micronesia, Fed. Sts.	0	0	0	0
Moldova	0	99.34463	0	99.34463
Monaco	0	0	0	0
Mongolia	95.84848	95.40971	-0.00458	-0.43877
Montenegro	97.96021	99.11542	0.011793	1.15521
Morocco	0	0	0	0
Mozambique	0	28.0707	0	28.0707
Myanmar	0	0	0	0
Namibia	50.70204	0	0	-50.702
Nepal	0	0	0	0
Netherlands	0	98.4706	0	98.4706
New Zealand	0	0	0	0
Nicaragua	0	0	0	0
Niger	0	0	0	0
Nigeria	0	0	0	0

Norway	0	99.95481	0	99.95481
Oman	57.36736	69.44403	0.210515	12.07667
Pakistan	0	58.22991	0	58.22991
Palau	0	0	0	0
Panama	76.38219	82.77547	0.083701	6.39328
Papua New Guinea	0	0	0	0
Paraguay	67.19394	67.9434	0.011154	0.74946
Peru	0	82.22293	0	82.22293
Philippines	79.55824	81.05412	0.018802	1.495877
Poland	97.99903	99.26581	0.012926	1.26678
Portugal	85.53582	91.42698	0.068874	5.891163
Qatar	0	74.88077	0	74.88077
Romania	97.34884	98.88591	0.015789	1.537068
Russian Federation	99.69062	99.55822	-0.00133	-0.1324
Rwanda	0	36.0947	0	36.0947
Samoa	96.12893	98.92645	0.029102	2.79752
San Marino	0	0	0	0
Sao Tome and Principe	0	0	0	0
Saudi Arabia	68.73505	77.77939	0.131583	9.044335
Senegal	0	25.86555	0	25.86555
Serbia	81.67883	95.78292	0.172677	14.10409
Seychelles	94.0644	0	0	-94.0644
Sierra Leone	0	0	0	0
Singapore	0	85.726	0	85.726
Slovak Republic	99.67335	99.79814	0.001252	0.124785
Slovenia	0	99.44121	0	99.44121
Solomon Islands	0	0	0	0
Somalia	0	0	0	0
South Africa	69.48791	78.40762	0.128363	8.919711
South Sudan	0	10.73225	0	10.73225
Spain	0	90.00006	0	90.00006
Sri Lanka	88.43692	0	0	-88.4369
St. Kitts and Nevis	0	0	0	0
St. Lucia	0	0	0	0
St. Vincent and the Grenadines	0	0	0	0
Sudan	0	0	0	0
Suriname	0	91.94998	0	91.94998
Swaziland	0	0	0	0
Sweden	0	100	0	100
Switzerland	0	100	0	100
Syrian Arab Republic	39.01759	74.74661	0.915716	35.72902
Tajikistan	98.33491	0	0	-98.3349
Tanzania	56.65922	71.22065	0.257	14.56143

Thailand	0	61.18225	0	61.18225
Timor-Leste	0	0	0	0
Togo	0	10.73225	0	10.73225
Tonga	100	95.98412	-0.04016	-4.01588
Trinidad and Tobago	0	95.88151	0	95.88151
Tunisia	0	0	0	0
Turkey	0	91.75652	0	91.75652
Turkmenistan	97.97322	0	0	-97.9732
Tuvalu	0	0	0	0
Uganda	40.18148	10.73225	-0.73291	-29.4492
Ukraine	98.68858	0	0	-98.6886
United Arab Emirates	0	73.17483	0	73.17483
United Kingdom	0	99.87889	0	99.87889
United States	0	98.61341	0	98.61341
Uruguay	90.66017	86.54938	-0.04534	-4.11079
Uzbekistan	0	100	0	100
Vanuatu	0	0	0	0
Venezuela, RB	69.53788	79.55674	0.144078	10.01886
Vietnam	0	0	0	0
Yemen, Rep.	0	0	0	0
Zambia	0	0	0	0
Zimbabwe	10.73225	10.73225	0	0
	25.13182	**44.04461**	**0.752544**	**18.91279**

(The World Bank Group, 2016)

The thirteenth through the sixteenth measurements calculated the annual primary completion rate averages, percentage of change, and shift for males that were twenty-five years or older between the 2007 to 2010 time period and the 2011 to 2014 time period for nations that reported annual primary completion rate data every year from 2007 to 2014 for 193 nations in the world with the exception of Nauru and the Vatican City State (Nations Online, 2016).

Country Name	2007-2010 Average	2011-2014 Average	% of Change	Male Primary Shift
Azerbaijan	98.77837	99.21944	0.004465	0.44107
Cyprus	95.58989	96.44445	0.00894	0.854555
Czech Republic	99.86695	99.82418	-0.00043	-0.04277
France	99.08428	98.26043	-0.00831	-0.82386

Germany	100	100	0	0
Latvia	99.8682	99.89827	0.000301	0.030068
Lithuania	98.75741	99.11855	0.003657	0.361138
Moldova	99.26884	99.42043	0.001527	0.151593
Netherlands	98.42074	98.57964	0.001614	0.158898
Peru	80.65589	84.98775	0.053708	4.331865
Portugal	91.25425	92.94617	0.018541	1.691925
Qatar	75.00436	77.76674	0.03683	2.762388
Romania	98.70972	99.06209	0.00357	0.35237
Singapore	84.01238	88.10106	0.048668	4.088683
Slovenia	99.03638	99.82	0.007912	0.783623
Turkey	90.90572	93.88951	0.032823	2.983785
	94.32584	**95.45867**	**0.01201**	**1.132833**

(The World Bank Group, 2016)

The seventeenth through the twentieth measurements calculated the annual lower secondary completion rate averages, percentage of change, and shift for females that were twenty-five years or older between the 1993 to 2003 time period and the 2004 and 2014 time period for 193 nations in the world with the exception of Nauru and the Vatican City State (Nations Online, 2016).

Country Name	1993-2003 Average	2004-2014 Average	% of Change	Female Lower Shift
Afghanistan	0	0	0	0
Albania	70.99655	82.04348	0.155598	11.04693
Algeria	0	30.21648	0	30.21648
Andorra	42.77512	54.43095	0.272491	11.65583
Angola	0	0	0	0
Antigua and Barbuda	0	0	0	0
Argentina	51.1467	0	-1	-51.1467
Armenia	89.97026	96.12444	0.068402	6.15418
Australia	0	91.78491	0	91.78491
Austria	0	98.66513	0	98.66513
Azerbaijan	90.00769	92.8611	0.031702	2.853411
Bahamas, The	91.63446	89.17299	-0.02686	-2.46147
Bahrain	56.94969	56.70442	-0.00431	-0.24527
Bangladesh	22.03034	0	0	-22.0303
Barbados	78.69389	0	0	-78.6939
Belarus	0	89.44789	0	89.44789

Belgium	0	77.1758	0	77.1758
Belize	0	54.16804	0	54.16804
Benin	8.42976	0	0	-8.42976
Bhutan	0	5.84356	0	5.84356
Bolivia	38.17161	41.47912	0.086648	3.307508
Bosnia and Herzegovina	0	44.85299	0	44.85299
Botswana	0	0	0	0
Brazil	0	51.03316	0	51.03316
Brunei Darussalam	0	0	0	0
Bulgaria	84.97125	91.52663	0.077148	6.555377
Burkina Faso	0	4.013517	0	4.013517
Burundi	0	0	0	0
Cambodia	0	10.03872	0	10.03872
Cameroon	0	26.36511	0	26.36511
Canada	0	0	0	0
Cabo Verde	0	0	0	0
Central African Republic	0	0	0	0
Chad	0	1.66286	0	1.66286
Chile	0	74.22733	0	74.22733
China	43.37749	58.65146	0.352117	15.27397
Colombia	0	47.05877	0	47.05877
Congo, Dem. Rep.	0	27.51626	0	27.51626
Congo, Rep.	0	0	0	0
Costa Rica	0	50.42519	0	50.42519
Cote d'Ivoire	0	0	0	0
Croatia	71.87345	85.16027	0.184864	13.28682
Cuba	65.83835	79.14892	0.20217	13.31057
Curacao	0	0	0	0
Cyprus	0	71.518	0	71.518
Czech Republic	0	99.80877	0	99.80877
Denmark	99.36601	98.97089	-0.00398	-0.39512
Djibouti	0	0	0	0
Dominica	29.94473	0	0	-29.9447
Dominican Republic	0	53.44526	0	53.44526
Ecuador	0	43.15469	0	43.15469
Egypt, Arab Rep.	0	0	0	0
El Salvador	0	35.55724	0	35.55724
Equatorial Guinea	0	0	0	0
Eritrea	0	0	0	0
Estonia	87.92752	0	0	-87.9275
Ethiopia	0	6.21464	0	6.21464
Fiji	43.49796	60.93365	0.400839	17.43569
Finland	0	0	0	0

France	0	75.74939	0	75.74939
Gabon	0	0	0	0
Gambia, The	0	0	0	0
Georgia	89.74452	95.42711	0.06332	5.68259
Germany	0	96.54086	0	96.54086
Ghana	0	45.20022	0	45.20022
Greece	0	56.754	0	56.754
Grenada	0	0	0	0
Guatemala	15.52663	23.47035	0.511619	7.943715
Guinea	0	0	0	0
Guinea-Bissau	0	0	0	0
Guyana	33.24209	0	0	-33.2421
Haiti	0	0	0	0
Honduras	0	27.63198	0	27.63198
Hungary	83.76087	95.95344	0.145564	12.19257
Iceland	0	95.09661	0	95.09661
India	0	0	0	0
Indonesia	0	37.97568	0	37.97568
Iran, Islamic Rep.	0	61.4348	0	61.4348
Iraq	0	0	0	0
Ireland	0	81.2636	0	81.2636
Israel	0	78.7853	0	78.7853
Italy	59.28407	67.46414	0.137981	8.180069
Jamaica	0	64.62962	0	64.62962
Japan	0	0	0	0
Jordan	40.49253	66.03171	0.630713	25.53918
Kazakhstan	78.95603	99.25005	0.257029	20.29402
Kenya	0	26.60682	0	26.60682
Kiribati	0	0	0	0
Korea, Dem. People's Rep.	0	0	0	0
Korea, Rep.	66.93947	74.04075	0.106085	7.101277
Kosovo	0	0	0	0
Kuwait	0	51.65531	0	51.65531
Kyrgyz Republic	86.5112	94.51887	0.092562	8.00767
Lao PDR	0	0	0	0
Latvia	0	98.59132	0	98.59132
Lebanon	0	53.15132	0	53.15132
Lesotho	0	24.64275	0	24.64275
Liberia	0	0	0	0
Libya	0	0	0	0
Liechtenstein	0	0	0	0
Lithuania	0	87.76694	0	87.76694
Luxembourg	100	94.85553	-0.05144	-5.14447

Macedonia, FYR	40.16013	0	0	-40.1601
Madagascar	0	0	0	0
Malawi	4.3736	0	0	-4.3736
Malaysia	51.69601	57.18413	0.106161	5.488117
Maldives	0	14.01297	0	14.01297
Mali	0	9.52604	0	9.52604
Malta	33.51878	65.29979	0.948155	31.78101
Marshall Islands	0	91.64423	0	91.64423
Mauritania	0	0	0	0
Mauritius	33.51878	49.79731	0.485654	16.27853
Mexico	37.39071	50.8545	0.360084	13.46379
Micronesia, Fed. Sts.	0	0	0	0
Moldova	0	92.45237	0	92.45237
Monaco	0	0	0	0
Mongolia	77.76004	85.29262	0.09687	7.53258
Montenegro	77.0193	84.38664	0.095656	7.36734
Morocco	0	0	0	0
Mozambique	0	12.23835	0	12.23835
Myanmar	0	0	0	0
Namibia	27.2332	0	0	-27.2332
Nepal	0	0	0	0
Netherlands	0	87.76705	0	87.76705
New Zealand	0	100	0	100
Nicaragua	0	0	0	0
Niger	0	0	0	0
Nigeria	0	0	0	0
Norway	0	99.65319	0	99.65319
Oman	32.74653	49.16803	0.501473	16.4215
Pakistan	0	19.83896	0	19.83896
Palau	0	0	0	0
Panama	49.15827	62.88883	0.279313	13.73056
Papua New Guinea	0	0	0	0
Paraguay	33.77283	37.00751	0.095778	3.234683
Peru	0	51.5824	0	51.5824
Philippines	50.35251	67.37976	0.338161	17.02725
Poland	0	78.56838	0	78.56838
Portugal	24.72621	40.14294	0.623498	15.41673
Qatar	0	64.5942	0	64.5942
Romania	74.30645	84.47082	0.13679	10.16437
Russian Federation	97.12966	92.26023	-0.05013	-4.86943
Rwanda	0	9.42537	0	9.42537
Samoa	0	0	0	0
San Marino	0	0	0	0

Sao Tome and Principe	0	31.77432	0	31.77432
Saudi Arabia	31.78774	51.70458	0.626557	19.91684
Senegal	0	7.12088	0	7.12088
Serbia	46.55145	80.69376	0.733432	34.14231
Seychelles	68.831	0	0	-68.831
Sierra Leone	0	0	0	0
Singapore	0	71.65167	0	71.65167
Slovak Republic	99.60803	99.11765	-0.00492	-0.49038
Slovenia	0	95.12426	0	95.12426
Solomon Islands	0	0	0	0
Somalia	0	0	0	0
South Africa	57.93032	67.49958	0.165186	9.569258
South Sudan	0	9.58302	0	9.58302
Spain	0	62.96744	0	62.96744
Sri Lanka	72.96786	72.66208	-0.00419	-0.30578
St. Kitts and Nevis	0	0	0	0
St. Lucia	0	48.94937	0	48.94937
St. Vincent and the Grenadines	0	0	0	0
Sudan	0	0	0	0
Suriname	0	54.60618	0	54.60618
Swaziland	0	0	0	0
Sweden	0	88.22103	0	88.22103
Switzerland	0	95.45387	0	95.45387
Syrian Arab Republic	25.64257	28.13899	0.097354	2.496417
Tajikistan	89.93707	0	0	-89.9371
Tanzania	4.16211	8.57324	1.05983	4.41113
Thailand	0	33.50768	0	33.50768
Timor-Leste	0	0	0	0
Togo	0	9.58302	0	9.58302
Tonga	72.47495	77.97245	0.075854	5.4975
Trinidad and Tobago	0	59.60144	0	59.60144
Tunisia	0	29.67432	0	29.67432
Turkey	0	31.08185	0	31.08185
Turkmenistan	88.1418	0	0	-88.1418
Tuvalu	0	0	0	0
Uganda	7.10351	9.58302	0.349054	2.47951
Ukraine	85.58295	0	0	-85.583
United Arab Emirates	0	70.85817	0	70.85817
United Kingdom	0	99.76682	0	99.76682
United States	0	94.76042	0	94.76042
Uruguay	52.00247	52.27286	0.0052	0.270394
Uzbekistan	0	99.86237	0	99.86237
Vanuatu	0	0	0	0

Country Name				
Venezuela, RB	15.485	56.1316	2.624902	40.6466
Vietnam	0	59.43264	0	59.43264
Yemen, Rep.	0	0	0	0
Zambia	0	42.60869	0	42.60869
Zimbabwe	9.58302	9.58302	0	0
	17.5892	**37.4272**	**1.127852**	**19.838**

(The World Bank Group, 2016)

The twenty-first through the twenty-fourth measurements calculated the annual lower secondary completion rate averages, percentage of change, and shift for females that were twenty-five years or older between the 2009 to 2011 time period and the 2012 to 2014 time period for nations that reported annual lower secondary completion rate data every year from 2009 to 2014 for 193 nations in the world with the exception of Nauru and the Vatican City State (Nations Online, 2016).

Country Name	2009-2011 Average	2012-2014 Average	% of Change	Female Lower Shift
Australia	93.11159333	92.24196	-0.00934	-0.86963
Belgium	76.9997	79.08718667	0.02711	2.087487
Bulgaria	91.69725333	93.03240333	0.01456	1.33515
Colombia	48.60156	55.39518	0.139782	6.79362
Cyprus	72.58147	76.67935333	0.056459	4.097883
Czech Republic	99.79939333	99.84220333	0.000429	0.04281
France	76.48574	78.87693333	0.031263	2.391193
Germany	96.28563333	96.42332	0.00143	0.137687
Israel	83.78648667	86.43759667	0.031641	2.65111
Latvia	99.09884667	99.27583	0.001786	0.176983
Lithuania	88.62379333	90.13152667	0.017013	1.507733
Moldova	92.12035333	94.37146667	0.024437	2.251113
Netherlands	87.845	87.76442	-0.00092	-0.08058
Peru	51.58199667	56.61208333	0.097516	5.030087
Poland	77.84695333	80.28706667	0.031345	2.440113
Portugal	41.70254333	48.92262	0.173133	7.220077
Qatar	59.11568333	69.12513333	0.16932	10.00945
Romania	84.14395667	86.27196333	0.02529	2.128007
Slovenia	94.29981333	96.10763	0.019171	1.807817
Sweden	86.52206667	88.48761667	0.022717	1.96555
Turkey	34.26779333	42.12342	0.229242	7.855627

United Kingdom	99.75072667	99.78291667	0.000323	0.03219
United States	94.89672333	95.32148333	0.004476	0.42476
Uruguay	51.44954667	54.38076	0.056973	2.931213

(The World Bank Group, 2016)

The twenty-fifth through the twenty-eighth measurements calculated the annual lower secondary completion rate averages, percentage of change, and shift for males that were twenty-five years or older between the 1993 to 2003 time period and the 2004 and 2014 time period for 193 nations in the world with the exception of Nauru and the Vatican City State (Nations Online, 2016).

Country Name	1993-2003 Average	2004-2014 Average	% of Change	Male Lower Shift
Afghanistan	0	0	0	0
Albania	80.57056	87.625	0.087556	7.05444
Algeria	0	41.1927	0	41.1927
Andorra	41.79567	54.65761	0.307734	12.86194
Angola	0	0	0	0
Antigua and Barbuda	0	0	0	0
Argentina	51.11123	0	0	-51.1112
Armenia	92.39198	97.16112	0.051619	4.76914
Australia	0	92.18618	0	92.18618
Austria	0	99.20062	0	99.20062
Azerbaijan	96.04223	97.02615	0.010245	0.983924
Bahamas, The	88.17584	89.09677	0.010444	0.92093
Bahrain	74.69296	54.00999	-0.27691	-20.683
Bangladesh	31.30774	0	0	-31.3077
Barbados	77.45673	0	0	-77.4567
Belarus	0	94.97328	0	94.97328
Belgium	0	82.63996	0	82.63996
Belize	0	54.60249	0	54.60249
Benin	21.21825	0	0	-21.2183
Bhutan	0	13.47972	0	13.47972
Bolivia	52.52847	51.69292	-0.01591	-0.83555
Bosnia and Herzegovina	0	69.91383	0	69.91383
Botswana	0	0	0	0
Brazil	0	48.80097	0	48.80097
Brunei Darussalam	0	0	0	0

Bulgaria	91.03967	94.81661	0.041487	3.776941
Burkina Faso	0	8.680067	0	8.680067
Burundi	0	0	0	0
Cambodia	0	22.82356	0	22.82356
Cameroon	0	46.87472	0	46.87472
Canada	0	0	0	0
Cabo Verde	0	0	0	0
Central African Republic	0	0	0	0
Chad	0	9.88933	0	9.88933
Chile	0	76.75274	0	76.75274
China	60.7806	71.85912	0.182271	11.07852
Colombia	0	46.36397	0	46.36397
Congo, Dem. Rep.	0	59.15372	0	59.15372
Congo, Rep.	0	0	0	0
Costa Rica	0	50.17776	0	50.17776
Cote d'Ivoire	0	0	0	0
Croatia	85.70537	93.77158	0.094116	8.06621
Cuba	71.78482	83.21731	0.159261	11.43249
Curacao	0	0	0	0
Cyprus	0	77.89974	0	77.89974
Czech Republic	0	99.79494	0	99.79494
Denmark	100	98.86182	-0.01138	-1.13818
Djibouti	0	0	0	0
Dominica	23.2228	0	0	-23.2228
Dominican Republic	0	51.4964	0	51.4964
Ecuador	0	43.40476	0	43.40476
Egypt, Arab Rep.	0	0	0	0
El Salvador	0	41.80678	0	41.80678
Equatorial Guinea	0	0	0	0
Eritrea	0	0	0	0
Estonia	91.20463	0	0	-91.2046
Ethiopia	0	14.06001	0	14.06001
Fiji	46.74672	59.70481	0.277198	12.95809
Finland	0	0	0	0
France	0	81.7189	0	81.7189
Gabon	0	0	0	0
Gambia, The	0	0	0	0
Georgia	92.76788	97.03727	0.046022	4.26939
Germany	0	97.21875	0	97.21875
Ghana	0	64.66431	0	64.66431
Greece	0	65.52182	0	65.52182
Grenada	0	0	0	0
Guatemala	18.9558	27.48691	0.450053	8.531108

Guinea	0	0	0	0
Guinea-Bissau	0	0	0	0
Guyana	29.03922	0	0	-29.0392
Haiti	0	0	0	0
Honduras	0	25.72676	0	25.72676
Hungary	91.50399	97.87019	0.069573	6.366196
Iceland	0	96.58503	0	96.58503
India	0	0	0	0
Indonesia	0	48.04933	0	48.04933
Iran, Islamic Rep.	0	67.2865	0	67.2865
Iraq	0	0	0	0
Ireland	0	78.03996	0	78.03996
Israel	0	84.98439	0	84.98439
Italy	70.11254	77.6609	0.107661	7.548361
Jamaica	0	56.55267	0	56.55267
Japan	0	0	0	0
Jordan	44.36744	76.17858	0.716993	31.81114
Kazakhstan	85.8605	99.4288	0.158027	13.5683
Kenya	0	35.3609	0	35.3609
Kiribati	0	0	0	0
Korea, Dem. People's Rep.	0	0	0	0
Korea, Rep.	83.49546	87.38539	0.046589	3.889933
Kosovo	0	0	0	0
Kuwait	0	46.80999	0	46.80999
Kyrgyz Republic	92.23183	96.93237	0.050964	4.70054
Lao PDR	0	0	0	0
Latvia	0	98.52603	0	98.52603
Lebanon	0	55.53895	0	55.53895
Lesotho	0	21.62086	0	21.62086
Liberia	0	0	0	0
Libya	0	0	0	0
Liechtenstein	0	0	0	0
Lithuania	0	93.42537	0	93.42537
Luxembourg	100	95.16282	-0.04837	-4.83718
Macedonia, FYR	55.60117	0	0	-55.6012
Madagascar	0	0	0	0
Malawi	12.92061	0	0	-12.9206
Malaysia	61.20166	63.83341	0.043001	2.631753
Maldives	0	17.76027	0	17.76027
Mali	0	12.15618	0	12.15618
Malta	44.9455	74.71934	0.662443	29.77384
Marshall Islands	0	92.46858	0	92.46858

Mauritania	0	0	0	0
Mauritius	44.9455	58.94835	0.311552	14.00285
Mexico	43.70714	55.79649	0.276599	12.08935
Micronesia, Fed. Sts.	0	0	0	0
Moldova	0	95.88778	0	95.88778
Monaco	0	0	0	0
Mongolia	82.80058	84.10076	0.015703	1.30018
Montenegro	90.60268	94.84259	0.046797	4.23991
Morocco	0	0	0	0
Mozambique	0	18.928	0	18.928
Myanmar	0	0	0	0
Namibia	30.0079	0	0	-30.0079
Nepal	0	0	0	0
Netherlands	0	91.28395	0	91.28395
New Zealand	0	100	0	100
Nicaragua	0	0	0	0
Niger	0	0	0	0
Nigeria	0	0	0	0
Norway	0	99.72573	0	99.72573
Oman	43.38039	55.13894	0.271057	11.75855
Pakistan	0	43.03413	0	43.03413
Palau	0	0	0	0
Panama	45.82588	60.06999	0.310831	14.24411
Papua New Guinea	0	0	0	0
Paraguay	36.00699	41.24122	0.145367	5.234228
Peru	0	62.03246	0	62.03246
Philippines	50.57205	65.25186	0.290275	14.67981
Poland	0	84.87758	0	84.87758
Portugal	27.37736	41.26903	0.507415	13.89167
Qatar	0	59.62808	0	59.62808
Romania	84.55765	91.26192	0.079286	6.704268
Russian Federation	97.10847	95.4295	-0.01729	-1.67897
Rwanda	0	15.39392	0	15.39392
Samoa	0	0	0	0
San Marino	0	0	0	0
Sao Tome and Principe	0	46.25484	0	46.25484
Saudi Arabia	50.30476	61.42515	0.22106	11.12039
Senegal	0	15.09953	0	15.09953
Serbia	61.91619	90.66455	0.464311	28.74836
Seychelles	70.46198	0	0	-70.462
Sierra Leone	0	0	0	0
Singapore	0	79.11476	0	79.11476
Slovak Republic	99.67335	99.52055	-0.00153	-0.1528

Slovenia	0	97.19286	0	97.19286
Solomon Islands	0	0	0	0
Somalia	0	0	0	0
South Africa	62.01586	71.20544	0.148181	9.189578
South Sudan	0	10.73225	0	10.73225
Spain	0	69.66108	0	69.66108
Sri Lanka	76.74546	75.50073	-0.01622	-1.24474
St. Kitts and Nevis	0	0	0	0
St. Lucia	0	42.57036	0	42.57036
St. Vincent and the Grenadines	0	0	0	0
Sudan	0	0	0	0
Suriname	0	57.88745	0	57.88745
Swaziland	0	0	0	0
Sweden	0	88.4309	0	88.4309
Switzerland	0	96.88569	0	96.88569
Syrian Arab Republic	23.85584	39.28151	0.64662	15.42567
Tajikistan	94.97341	0	0	-94.9734
Tanzania	7.98408	13.74334	0.721343	5.75926
Thailand	0	39.51265	0	39.51265
Timor-Leste	0	0	0	0
Togo	0	10.73225	0	10.73225
Tonga	75.78888	79.65817	0.051054	3.86929
Trinidad and Tobago	0	59.79066	0	59.79066
Tunisia	0	42.34073	0	42.34073
Turkey	0	50.93213	0	50.93213
Turkmenistan	93.62299	0	0	-93.623
Tuvalu	0	0	0	0
Uganda	16.32346	10.73225	-0.34253	-5.59121
Ukraine	92.28501	0	0	-92.285
United Arab Emirates	0	60.05529	0	60.05529
United Kingdom	0	99.87889	0	99.87889
United States	0	94.3736	0	94.3736
Uruguay	49.50006	49.25476	-0.00496	-0.24529
Uzbekistan	0	99.92466	0	99.92466
Vanuatu	0	0	0	0
Venezuela, RB	34.66135	51.23337	0.478112	16.57202
Vietnam	0	71.21181	0	71.21181
Yemen, Rep.	0	0	0	0
Zambia	0	60.09096	0	60.09096
Zimbabwe	10.73225	10.73225	0	0
	19.47418	**40.27538**	**1.068142**	**20.8012**

The twenty-ninth through the thirty-second measurements calculated the annual lower secondary completion rate averages, percentage of change, and shift for males that were twenty-five years or older between the 2009 to 2011 time period and the 2012 to 2014 time period for nations that reported annual lower secondary completion rate data every year from 2009 to 2014 for 193 nations in the world with the exception of Nauru and the Vatican City State (Nations Online, 2016).

Country Name	2009-2011 Average	2012-2014 Average	% of Change	Male Lower Shift
Australia	92.91859	92.41316	-0.00544	-0.50543
Azerbaijan	97.42657	97.49529	0.000705	0.068717
Belgium	82.64548	83.88496	0.014998	1.23948
Bulgaria	94.82359	95.67211	0.008948	0.848523
Colombia	47.3247	54.97217	0.161596	7.647467
Cyprus	79.31712	81.82612	0.031633	2.509
Czech Republic	99.8189	99.77685	-0.00042	-0.04205
France	82.12695	84.48639	0.028729	2.359433
Germany	97.03399	97.062	0.000289	0.02801
Hungary	98.51601	98.47359	-0.00043	-0.04242
Israel	86.76597	89.27546	0.028923	2.509493
Latvia	99.01218	99.14096	0.001301	0.12878
Lithuania	93.84336	94.95899	0.011888	1.11563
Moldova	95.78555	96.96072	0.012269	1.17517
Netherlands	91.15784	91.39822	0.002637	0.24038
Peru	63.14959	66.5928	0.054525	3.44321
Poland	84.26315	86.23316	0.023379	1.970013
Portugal	42.32041	49.78046	0.176275	7.460043
Qatar	53.2694	65.4127	0.22796	12.14329
Romania	91.01586	92.26409	0.013714	1.248227
Singapore	79.76174	81.5707	0.02268	1.80896
Slovenia	97.14553	98.19465	0.010799	1.049117
Sweden	87.64261	89.34992	0.01948	1.707313
Turkey	54.50663	63.99133	0.17401	9.484697
United Kingdom	99.8726	99.88517	0.000126	0.01257
United States	94.56285	94.96602	0.004263	0.403167
Uruguay	48.6763	50.82466	0.044136	2.148357
	82.7668	**85.06899**	**0.027815**	**2.30219**

The thirty-third through the thirty-sixth measurements calculated the annual upper secondary completion rate averages, percentage of change, and shift for females that were twenty-five years or older between the 1993 to 2003 time period and the 2004 and 2014 time period for 193 nations in the world with the exception of Nauru and the Vatican City State (Nations Online, 2016).

Country Name	1993-2003 Average	2004-2014 Average	% of Change	Female Upper Shift
Afghanistan	0	0	0	0
Albania	32.11785	39.50324	0.229946	7.385387
Algeria	0	14.69867	0	14.69867
Andorra	0	47.58965	0	47.58965
Angola	0	0	0	0
Antigua and Barbuda	0	0	0	0
Argentina	39.92194	0	0	-39.9219
Armenia	81.07005	90.36633	0.11467	9.29628
Australia	0	67.20567	0	67.20567
Austria	0	68.11857	0	68.11857
Azerbaijan	78.75169	83.5915	0.061457	4.83981
Bahamas, The	74.66477	82.45938	0.104395	7.79461
Bahrain	45.96088	45.20874	-0.01636	-0.75214
Bangladesh	13.3621	0	0	-13.3621
Barbados	25.40199	0	0	-25.402
Belarus	0	82.4668	0	82.4668
Belgium	0	59.96306	0	59.96306
Belize	0	37.27061	0	37.27061
Benin	0	0	0	0
Bhutan	0	2.93026	0	2.93026
Bolivia	32.33836	34.15689	0.056234	1.81853
Bosnia and Herzegovina	0	34.94313	0	34.94313
Botswana	0	0	0	0
Brazil	0	37.66311	0	37.66311
Brunei Darussalam	0	0	0	0
Bulgaria	57.86402	68.06165	0.176234	10.19763
Burkina Faso	0	1.342743	0	1.342743
Burundi	0	0	0	0
Cambodia	0	2.750243	0	2.750243
Cameroon	0	11.47701	0	11.47701

Country				
Canada	70.56536	80.9313	0.146898	10.36594
Cabo Verde	0	0	0	0
Central African Republic	0	0	0	0
Chad	0	0	0	0
Chile	0	52.79102	0	52.79102
China	0	19.19593	0	19.19593
Colombia	0	38.92589	0	38.92589
Congo, Dem. Rep.	0	10.2602	0	10.2602
Congo, Rep.	0	0	0	0
Costa Rica	0	36.97144	0	36.97144
Cote d'Ivoire	0	0	0	0
Croatia	50.45654	63.19987	0.252561	12.74333
Cuba	40.16478	57.14484	0.42276	16.98006
Curacao	0	0	0	0
Cyprus	0	61.81071	0	61.81071
Czech Republic	0	82.2344	0	82.2344
Denmark	99.36601	76.25157	-0.23262	-23.1144
Djibouti	0	0	0	0
Dominica	10.35547	0	0	-10.3555
Dominican Republic	0	34.98111	0	34.98111
Ecuador	0	34.99626	0	34.99626
Egypt, Arab Rep.	0	0	0	0
El Salvador	0	23.92108	0	23.92108
Equatorial Guinea	0	0	0	0
Eritrea	0	0	0	0
Estonia	72.05366	88.4909	0.228125	16.43724
Ethiopia	0	5.092015	0	5.092015
Fiji	23.74354	39.56132	0.666193	15.81778
Finland	63.70908	69.61286	0.092668	5.903777
France	0	58.42743	0	58.42743
Gabon	0	0	0	0
Gambia, The	0	0	0	0
Georgia	82.25921	90.4345	0.099384	8.17529
Germany	0	74.16461	0	74.16461
Ghana	0	14.6786	0	14.6786
Greece	0	48.77949	0	48.77949
Grenada	0	0	0	0
Guatemala	12.23205	17.5896	0.437992	5.357545
Guinea	0	0	0	0
Guinea-Bissau	0	0	0	0
Guyana	33.24209	0	0	-33.2421
Haiti	0	0	0	0
Honduras	0	20.19063	0	20.19063

Hungary	48.98694	70.23659	0.433782	21.24965
Iceland	0	54.83571	0	54.83571
India	0	0	0	0
Indonesia	0	23.86699	0	23.86699
Iran, Islamic Rep.	0	42.07386	0	42.07386
Iraq	0	0	0	0
Ireland	0	66.50633	0	66.50633
Israel	0	78.94069	0	78.94069
Italy	33.82684	42.67672	0.261623	8.849875
Jamaica	0	0	0	0
Japan	0	79.31059	0	79.31059
Jordan	1.31173	40.10516	29.57425	38.79343
Kazakhstan	68.32531	96.43464	0.411404	28.10933
Kenya	0	19.96241	0	19.96241
Kiribati	0	0	0	0
Korea, Dem. People's Rep.	0	0	0	0
Korea, Rep.	51.29833	62.29685	0.214403	10.99852
Kosovo	0	0	0	0
Kuwait	0	32.11166	0	32.11166
Kyrgyz Republic	74.72243	87.08672	0.16547	12.36429
Lao PDR	0	0	0	0
Latvia	0	85.47575	0	85.47575
Lebanon	0	32.51167	0	32.51167
Lesotho	0	14.19079	0	14.19079
Liberia	0	0	0	0
Libya	0	0	0	0
Liechtenstein	0	0	0	0
Lithuania	0	77.19113	0	77.19113
Luxembourg	42.47132	70.46072	0.659019	27.98941
Macedonia, FYR	0	0	0	0
Madagascar	0	0	0	0
Malawi	2.38688	0	0	-2.38688
Malaysia	33.44365	41.32029	0.23552	7.876643
Maldives	0	4.06645	0	4.06645
Mali	0	5.934295	0	5.934295
Malta	17.12125	25.062	0.463795	7.940751
Marshall Islands	0	67.58212	0	67.58212
Mauritania	0	0	0	0
Mauritius	17.12125	39.80235	1.324734	22.6811
Mexico	15.17352	27.9879	0.844522	12.81438
Micronesia, Fed. Sts.	0	0	0	0
Moldova	0	71.73579	0	71.73579
Monaco	0	0	0	0

Mongolia	55.77695	71.14128	0.27546	15.36433
Montenegro	55.60899	65.23196	0.173047	9.62297
Morocco	0	0	0	0
Mozambique	0	3.98379	0	3.98379
Myanmar	0	0	0	0
Namibia	16.29633	0	0	-16.2963
Nepal	0	0	0	0
Netherlands	0	62.32301	0	62.32301
New Zealand	0	68.30561	0	68.30561
Nicaragua	0	0	0	0
Niger	0	0	0	0
Nigeria	0	0	0	0
Norway	0	74.41185	0	74.41185
Oman	26.90695	41.01255	0.524236	14.1056
Pakistan	0	14.17903	0	14.17903
Palau	0	0	0	0
Panama	35.79741	45.81955	0.279968	10.02214
Papua New Guinea	0	0	0	0
Paraguay	23.95648	28.31322	0.181861	4.356738
Peru	0	45.44267	0	45.44267
Philippines	35.75606	56.52089	0.580736	20.76483
Poland	68.04301	78.42924	0.152642	10.38623
Portugal	16.37108	26.83846	0.639382	10.46738
Qatar	0	55.07546	0	55.07546
Romania	45.15379	58.69916	0.299983	13.54537
Russian Federation	89.41041	83.45717	-0.06658	-5.95324
Rwanda	0	6.43228	0	6.43228
Samoa	65.31117	74.63024	0.142687	9.31907
San Marino	0	0	0	0
Sao Tome and Principe	0	0	0	0
Saudi Arabia	23.49621	38.94282	0.657409	15.44661
Senegal	0	3.74968	0	3.74968
Serbia	0	58.48444	0	58.48444
Seychelles	44.1771	0	0	-44.1771
Sierra Leone	0	0	0	0
Singapore	0	61.51165	0	61.51165
Slovak Republic	42.86414	80.81972	0.885486	37.95558
Slovenia	0	71.50789	0	71.50789
Solomon Islands	0	0	0	0
Somalia	0	0	0	0
South Africa	39.04083	53.48549	0.369988	14.44465
South Sudan	0	9.58302	0	9.58302
Spain	0	41.6041	0	41.6041

Sri Lanka	55.60683	0	0	-55.6068
St. Kitts and Nevis	0	0	0	0
St. Lucia	0	42.83393	0	42.83393
St. Vincent and the Grenadines	0	0	0	0
Sudan	0	0	0	0
Suriname	0	17.02886	0	17.02886
Swaziland	0	0	0	0
Sweden	0	78.29505	0	78.29505
Switzerland	0	78.41908	0	78.41908
Syrian Arab Republic	6.8143	17.94278	1.633107	11.12848
Tajikistan	73.63909	0	0	-73.6391
Tanzania	0.94738	2.28588	1.412844	1.3385
Thailand	0	24.22999	0	24.22999
Timor-Leste	0	0	0	0
Togo	0	9.58302	0	9.58302
Tonga	0	38.49962	0	38.49962
Trinidad and Tobago	0	56.58991	0	56.58991
Tunisia	0	0	0	0
Turkey	0	21.58719	0	21.58719
Turkmenistan	73.18074	0	0	-73.1807
Tuvalu	0	0	0	0
Uganda	3.90654	9.58302	1.453071	5.67648
Ukraine	71.11248	0	0	-71.1125
United Arab Emirates	0	59.84927	0	59.84927
United Kingdom	0	80.58114	0	80.58114
United States	0	87.28365	0	87.28365
Uruguay	36.63955	29.97522	-0.18189	-6.66433
Uzbekistan	0	89.76049	0	89.76049
Vanuatu	0	0	0	0
Venezuela, RB	11.73233	42.83311	2.650861	31.10078
Vietnam	0	21.43751	0	21.43751
Yemen, Rep.	0	0	0	0
Zambia	0	23.25497	0	23.25497
Zimbabwe	9.58302	9.58302	0	0
	12.81306	**29.50023**	**1.302357**	**16.68717**

(The World Bank Group, 2016)

The thirty-seventh through fortieth measurements calculated the annual upper secondary completion rate averages, percentage of change, and shift for females that were twenty-five years or older between the 2009 to 2011 time period and the 2012 to 2014 time period for nations that reported annual upper secondary completion rate data every year from 2009 to 2014 for 193 nations in the world with the exception of Nauru and the Vatican City State (Nations Online, 2016).

Country Name	2009-2011 Average	2012-2014 Average	% of Change	Female Upper Shift
Australia	70.49	71.64	0.02	1.15
Austria	68.79	70.63	0.03	1.84
Azerbaijan	85.48	85.48	0.00	0.00
Belgium	59.97	62.23	0.04	2.26
Bulgaria	67.82	71.74	0.06	3.92
Colombia	40.18	43.33	0.08	3.16
Cyprus	62.74	67.47	0.08	4.73
Czech Republic	82.51	84.55	0.02	2.04
Denmark	73.91	76.13	0.03	2.21
France	58.86	63.22	0.07	4.36
Germany	75.17	77.16	0.03	1.99
Hungary	71.74	73.02	0.02	1.27
Latvia	87.27	89.28	0.02	2.00
Lithuania	78.07	80.26	0.03	2.19
Luxembourg	70.96	74.74	0.05	3.78
Moldova	72.02	72.29	0.00	0.27
Netherlands	62.30	64.56	0.04	2.27
Peru	46.20	51.24	0.11	5.04
Poland	77.75	80.08	0.03	2.33
Portugal	27.03	33.62	0.24	6.58
Qatar	51.30	56.60	0.10	5.30
Romania	58.31	59.65	0.02	1.34
Singapore	62.22	65.99	0.06	3.77
Slovenia	72.34	75.08	0.04	2.74
Sweden	78.10	75.36	-0.04	-2.74
Turkey	23.48	27.26	0.16	3.78
United Kingdom	83.91	77.25	-0.08	-6.67
United States	87.61	88.51	0.01	0.89
Uruguay	30.03	31.02	0.03	0.99
65.05	**67.22**	**0.03**	**2.17**

(The World Bank Group, 2016)

The forty-first through the forty-fourth measurements calculated the annual upper secondary completion rate averages, percentage of change, and shift for males that were twenty-five years or older between the 1993 to 2003 time period and the 2004 and 2014 time period for 193 nations in the world with the exception of Nauru and the Vatican City State (Nations Online, 2016).

Country Name	1993-2003 Average	2004-2014 Average	% of Change	Male Upper Shift
Afghanistan	0	0	0	0
Albania	42.0749	46.52444	0.105753	4.44954
Algeria	0	18.3592	0	18.3592
Andorra	0	48.08442	0	48.08442
Angola	0	0	0	0
Antigua and Barbuda	0	0	0	0
Argentina	36.39582	0	0	-36.3958
Armenia	82.19042	90.0856	0.09606	7.89518
Australia	0	73.13469	0	73.13469
Austria	0	84.0218	0	84.0218
Azerbaijan	88.93218	91.26991	0.026287	2.337734
Bahamas, The	66.24524	81.22307	0.226097	14.97783
Bahrain	51.70949	40.59559	-0.21493	-11.1139
Bangladesh	20.82129	0	0	-20.8213
Barbados	22.89339	0	0	-22.8934
Belarus	0	87.84233	0	87.84233
Belgium	0	64.14448	0	64.14448
Belize	0	36.37405	0	36.37405
Benin	0	0	0	0
Bhutan	0	8.1684	0	8.1684
Bolivia	44.01234	41.6958	-0.05263	-2.31654
Bosnia and Herzegovina	0	47.92492	0	47.92492
Botswana	0	0	0	0
Brazil	0	34.58556	0	34.58556
Brunei Darussalam	0	0	0	0
Bulgaria	61.21908	71.63837	0.170197	10.41929
Burkina Faso	0	3.732127	0	3.732127
Burundi	0	0	0	0
Cambodia	0	8.17409	0	8.17409
Cameroon	0	25.39948	0	25.39948
Canada	71.4653	81.23237	0.136669	9.76707
Cabo Verde	0	0	0	0
Central African Republic	0	0	0	0

Chad	0	0	0	0
Chile	0	54.39223	0	54.39223
China	0	25.37281	0	25.37281
Colombia	0	38.65153	0	38.65153
Congo, Dem. Rep.	0	30.56529	0	30.56529
Congo, Rep.	0	0	0	0
Costa Rica	0	35.93941	0	35.93941
Cote d'Ivoire	0	0	0	0
Croatia	69.99107	79.12711	0.130532	9.13604
Cuba	40.54679	57.67536	0.42244	17.12857
Curacao	0	0	0	0
Cyprus	0	67.55813	0	67.55813
Czech Republic	0	93.3572	0	93.3572
Denmark	84.52332	77.24625	-0.0861	-7.27707
Djibouti	0	0	0	0
Dominica	11.18336	0	0	-11.1834
Dominican Republic	0	29.42702	0	29.42702
Ecuador	0	35.51566	0	35.51566
Egypt, Arab Rep.	0	0	0	0
El Salvador	0	26.75186	0	26.75186
Equatorial Guinea	0	0	0	0
Eritrea	0	0	0	0
Estonia	70.69253	85.02093	0.202686	14.3284
Ethiopia	0	11.15023	0	11.15023
Fiji	27.40953	39.10955	0.42686	11.70002
Finland	65.14142	69.52552	0.067301	4.384101
France	0	65.24321	0	65.24321
Gabon	0	0	0	0
Gambia, The	0	0	0	0
Georgia	85.37539	92.79278	0.08688	7.417385
Germany	0	86.986	0	86.986
Ghana	0	27.24011	0	27.24011
Greece	0	54.10842	0	54.10842
Grenada	0	0	0	0
Guatemala	14.45439	19.72035	0.364315	5.265958
Guinea	0	0	0	0
Guinea-Bissau	0	0	0	0
Guyana	29.03922	0	0	-29.0392
Haiti	0	0	0	0
Honduras	0	18.07505	0	18.07505
Hungary	62.23713	79.05853	0.270279	16.8214

Iceland	0	66.59989	0	66.59989
India	0	0	0	0
Indonesia	0	31.48456	0	31.48456
Iran, Islamic Rep.	0	43.96299	0	43.96299
Iraq	0	0	0	0
Ireland	0	59.60415	0	59.60415
Israel	0	78.89067	0	78.89067
Italy	37.23555	45.62349	0.225267	8.387944
Jamaica	0	0	0	0
Japan	0	82.05399	0	82.05399
Jordan	1.5115	45.98222	29.42158	44.47072
Kazakhstan	73.16227	96.18498	0.31468	23.02271
Kenya	0	29.08395	0	29.08395
Kiribati	0	0	0	0
Korea, Dem. People's Rep.	0	0	0	0
Korea, Rep.	70.15933	77.03438	0.097992	6.875055
Kosovo	0	0	0	0
Kuwait	0	25.01573	0	25.01573
Kyrgyz Republic	79.43655	89.72533	0.129522	10.28878
Lao PDR	0	0	0	0
Latvia	0	81.04462	0	81.04462
Lebanon	0	33.38732	0	33.38732
Lesotho	0	13.38598	0	13.38598
Liberia	0	0	0	0
Libya	0	0	0	0
Liechtenstein	0	0	0	0
Lithuania	0	82.11668	0	82.11668
Luxembourg	47.88487	78.49775	0.639302	30.61288
Macedonia, FYR	0	0	0	0
Madagascar	0	0	0	0
Malawi	8.13841	0	0	-8.13841
Malaysia	39.33063	43.92904	0.116917	4.59841
Maldives	0	6.41592	0	6.41592
Mali	0	7.835345	0	7.835345
Malta	23.82571	32.74805	0.374484	8.922339
Marshall Islands	0	72.00105	0	72.00105
Mauritania	0	0	0	0
Mauritius	23.82571	47.58339	0.997145	23.75768
Mexico	22.31684	31.64114	0.417815	9.324301
Micronesia, Fed. Sts.	0	0	0	0
Moldova	0	77.31721	0	77.31721

Monaco	0	0	0	0
Mongolia	50.83163	63.80099	0.255144	12.96936
Montenegro	74.25948	80.43216	0.083123	6.17268
Morocco	0	0	0	0
Mozambique	0	6.61647	0	6.61647
Myanmar	0	0	0	0
Namibia	19.01573	0	0	-19.0157
Nepal	0	0	0	0
Netherlands	0	71.65427	0	71.65427
New Zealand	0	71.83723	0	71.83723
Nicaragua	0	0	0	0
Niger	0	0	0	0
Nigeria	0	0	0	0
Norway	0	76.98661	0	76.98661
Oman	30.17998	41.41526	0.372276	11.23528
Pakistan	0	29.23275	0	29.23275
Palau	0	0	0	0
Panama	31.56519	40.14485	0.271808	8.57966
Papua New Guinea	0	0	0	0
Paraguay	24.20457	29.89973	0.235293	5.695158
Peru	0	54.64286	0	54.64286
Philippines	35.66038	53.82659	0.509423	18.16621
Poland	76.23548	84.67199	0.110664	8.436513
Portugal	15.96893	24.41648	0.528999	8.447552
Qatar	0	40.97032	0	40.97032
Romania	60.91889	71.2246	0.169171	10.30571
Russian Federation	88.7068	85.88612	-0.0318	-2.82068
Rwanda	0	10.73664	0	10.73664
Samoa	60.87452	70.3925	0.156354	9.51798
San Marino	0	0	0	0
Sao Tome and Principe	0	0	0	0
Saudi Arabia	34.59194	43.16414	0.247809	8.5722
Senegal	0	9.244677	0	9.244677
Serbia	0	72.58275	0	72.58275
Seychelles	47.99813	0	0	-47.9981
Sierra Leone	0	0	0	0
Singapore	0	67.15757	0	67.15757
Slovak Republic	40.50427	90.37475	1.23124	49.87048
Slovenia	0	82.255	0	82.255
Solomon Islands	0	0	0	0
Somalia	0	0	0	0

South Africa	42.80565	57.19662	0.336193	14.39097
South Sudan	0	10.73225	0	10.73225
Spain	0	44.46156	0	44.46156
Sri Lanka	56.62371	0	0	-56.6237
St. Kitts and Nevis	0	0	0	0
St. Lucia	0	37.81667	0	37.81667
St. Vincent and the Grenadines	0	0	0	0
Sudan	0	0	0	0
Suriname	0	16.33303	0	16.33303
Swaziland	0	0	0	0
Sweden	0	76.98072	0	76.98072
Switzerland	0	88.06241	0	88.06241
Syrian Arab Republic	14.30052	25.38688	0.775242	11.08636
Tajikistan	84.44608	0	0	-84.4461
Tanzania	2.36253	4.62521	0.957736	2.26268
Thailand	0	26.77551	0	26.77551
Timor-Leste	0	0	0	0
Togo	0	10.73225	0	10.73225
Tonga	0	38.98272	0	38.98272
Trinidad and Tobago	0	57.17451	0	57.17451
Tunisia	0	0	0	0
Turkey	0	34.5048	0	34.5048
Turkmenistan	81.30136	0	0	-81.3014
Tuvalu	0	0	0	0
Uganda	9.22589	10.73225	0.163275	1.50636
Ukraine	78.37256	0	0	-78.3726
United Arab Emirates	0	42.99069	0	42.99069
United Kingdom	0	84.00935	0	84.00935
United States	0	86.33496	0	86.33496
Uruguay	32.00841	23.92674	-0.25249	-8.08167
Uzbekistan	0	93.39608	0	93.39608
Vanuatu	0	0	0	0
Venezuela, RB	33.08098	36.73321	0.110403	3.652233
Vietnam	0	30.41423	0	30.41423
Yemen, Rep.	0	0	0	0
Zambia	0	39.16367	0	39.16367
Zimbabwe	10.73225	10.73225	0	0
	14.05263	**31.73439**	**1.258253**	**17.68176**

(The World Bank Group, 2016)

The forty-fifth through forty-eighth measurements calculated the annual upper secondary completion rate averages, percentage of change, and shift for males that were twenty-five years or older between the 2009 to 2011 time period and the 2012 to 2014 time period for nations that reported annual upper secondary completion rate data every year from 2009 to 2014 for 193 nations in the world with the exception of Nauru and the Vatican City State (Nations Online, 2016).

Country Name	2009-2011 Average	2012-2014 Average	% of Change	Male Upper Shift
Australia	74.66476	74.88209	0.002911	0.217323
Austria	84.34044	84.81573	0.005635	0.475293
Azerbaijan	92.08861	92.23608	0.001601	0.147473
Bulgaria	71.38754	75.23987	0.053964	3.852327
Colombia	39.34838	43.01284	0.093129	3.664457
Cyprus	68.80258	71.62335	0.040998	2.82077
Czech Republic	93.64027	93.97083	0.00353	0.33056
Denmark	77.79378	74.4421	-0.04308	-3.35168
France	65.44005	69.50646	0.062139	4.06641
Germany	87.52504	88.06098	0.006123	0.535933
Latvia	82.156	84.30774	0.026191	2.15174
Lithuania	83.641	85.11841	0.017664	1.47741
Moldova	77.77338	76.99032	-0.01007	-0.78306
Netherlands	70.90515	72.97083	0.029133	2.065683
Peru	56.31914	60.40653	0.072575	4.087387
Portugal	24.48113	30.20476	0.233798	5.72363
Qatar	37.99399	40.79022	0.073597	2.79623
Singapore	68.1902	71.60257	0.050042	3.41237
Slovenia	83.61141	84.44839	0.01001	0.836983
Sweden	77.14701	76.25183	-0.0116	-0.89519
Turkey	36.3511	40.74616	0.120906	4.395067
69.21909	**71.02991**	**0.026161**	**1.810815**

(The World Bank Group, 2016)

The forty-ninth through the fifty-second measurements calculated the annual employment to population ratio averages, percentage of change, and shift for females who were fifteen years or older between the 1993 to 2003 time period and the 2004 and 2014 time period for 193 nations in the world with the exception of Nauru and the Vatican City State (Nations Online, 2016).

Country Name	1993-2003 Average	2004-2014 Average	% of Change	Female Employment Shift
Afghanistan	11.45	12.97	0.13	1.52
Albania	42.18	39.7	-0.06	-2.48
Algeria	6.05	11.35	0.88	5.3
Andorra	0	0	0	0
Angola	62.89	58.55	-0.07	-4.34
Antigua and Barbuda	0	0	0	0
Argentina	34.76	43.02	0.24	8.25
Armenia	43.29	38.71	-0.11	-4.58
Australia	49.99	55.15	0.1	5.16
Austria	46.33	50.73	0.09	4.4
Azerbaijan	52.03	57.25	0.1	5.23
Bahamas, The	59.39	59.77	0.01	0.38
Bahrain	31.03	35.5	0.14	4.47
Bangladesh	54.73	53.43	-0.02	-1.3
Barbados	51.91	58.05	0.12	6.15
Belarus	51.41	47.73	-0.07	-3.68
Belgium	37.28	42.68	0.14	5.4
Belize	31.61	39.39	0.25	7.78
Benin	61.94	66.24	0.07	4.3
Bhutan	49.97	62.73	0.26	12.75
Bolivia	54.65	60.07	0.1	5.42
Bosnia and Herzegovina	24.47	23	-0.06	-1.47
Botswana	52.49	55.44	0.06	2.95
Brazil	48.75	52.95	0.09	4.2
Brunei Darussalam	50.75	51.78	0.02	1.04
Bulgaria	40.37	42.81	0.06	2.44
Burkina Faso	75.34	75.35	0	0.02
Burundi	79.42	76.83	-0.03	-2.59
Cambodia	74.52	77.63	0.04	3.11
Cameroon	55.89	59.75	0.07	3.86
Canada	53.31	57.56	0.08	4.25
Cabo Verde	39.73	44.01	0.11	4.28
Central African Republic	65.36	66.74	0.02	1.37

Country				
Chad	59.58	59.25	-0.01	-0.33
Chile	31.93	39.95	0.25	8.02
China	68.32	62.48	-0.09	-5.84
Colombia	35.3	45.82	0.3	10.52
Congo, Dem. Rep.	63.61	64.05	0.01	0.44
Congo, Rep.	59.39	63.31	0.07	3.92
Costa Rica	35.05	40.84	0.17	5.79
Cote d'Ivoire	45.93	49.58	0.08	3.65
Croatia	39.04	39.41	0.01	0.37
Cuba	35.04	40.5	0.16	5.46
Curacao	0	0	0	0
Cyprus	43.66	51.14	0.17	7.47
Czech Republic	47.83	46.05	-0.04	-1.78
Denmark	55.23	56.55	0.02	1.32
Djibouti	0	0	0	0
Dominica	0	0	0	0
Dominican Republic	34.41	38.42	0.12	4.01
Ecuador	43.7	50.66	0.16	6.96
Egypt, Arab Rep.	15.06	16.83	0.12	1.76
El Salvador	41.54	44.38	0.07	2.85
Equatorial Guinea	75.41	74.62	-0.01	-0.79
Eritrea	68.1	73.01	0.07	4.91
Estonia	48.42	50.67	0.05	2.25
Ethiopia	65.11	71.96	0.11	6.85
Fiji	34.34	33.61	-0.02	-0.73
Finland	48.98	52.19	0.07	3.21
France	41.95	45.64	0.09	3.68
Gabon	41.98	40.1	-0.04	-1.88
Gambia, The	65.16	66.53	0.02	1.36
Georgia	50.85	48.23	-0.05	-2.63
Germany	44.19	48.48	0.1	4.29
Ghana	64.92	64.5	-0.01	-0.42
Greece	32.68	34.89	0.07	2.21
Grenada	0	0	0	0
Guatemala	40.15	45.95	0.14	5.8
Guinea	62.28	63.78	0.02	1.5
Guinea-Bissau	57.29	62.51	0.09	5.22
Guyana	32.49	35.21	0.08	2.72
Haiti	50.45	54.7	0.08	4.25
Honduras	37.97	39.09	0.03	1.12
Hungary	38.27	39.65	0.04	1.38

Iceland	67.7	67.44	0	-0.26
India	33.44	29.7	-0.11	-3.74
Indonesia	46.5	45.95	-0.01	-0.55
Iran, Islamic Rep.	10.22	13.82	0.35	3.6
Iraq	8.57	10.65	0.24	2.07
Ireland	40.29	48.91	0.21	8.62
Israel	42.11	49.05	0.16	6.94
Italy	29.62	34.48	0.16	4.86
Jamaica	48.68	47.86	-0.02	-0.82
Japan	47.74	46.58	-0.02	-1.15
Jordan	9.08	11.16	0.23	2.08
Kazakhstan	55.2	61.27	0.11	6.07
Kenya	57.32	54.71	-0.05	-2.61
Kiribati	0	0	0	0
Korea, Dem. People's Rep.	72.66	70.35	-0.03	-2.32
Korea, Rep.	47.15	48.35	0.03	1.19
Kosovo	0	0	0	0
Kuwait	42.33	42.7	0.01	0.37
Kyrgyz Republic	51.04	49.87	-0.02	-1.16
Lao PDR	77.85	75.85	-0.03	-1.99
Latvia	45.61	47.93	0.05	2.32
Lebanon	16.87	19.29	0.14	2.42
Lesotho	40.53	38.36	-0.05	-2.16
Liberia	55.59	55.87	0.01	0.28
Libya	17.61	21.65	0.23	4.04
Liechtenstein	0	0	0	0
Lithuania	47.23	48.25	0.02	1.02
Luxembourg	37.52	45.21	0.2	7.69
Macedonia, FYR	27.75	28.38	0.02	0.63
Madagascar	80.41	81.82	0.02	1.41
Malawi	69.79	75.92	0.09	6.13
Malaysia	41.7	42.76	0.03	1.06
Maldives	27.39	43.17	0.58	15.78
Mali	32.25	40.49	0.26	8.24
Malta	26.94	31.35	0.16	4.42
Marshall Islands	0	0	0	0
Mauritania	15.25	19.13	0.25	3.88
Mauritius	34.66	36.45	0.05	1.79
Mexico	36.55	41.3	0.13	4.75
Micronesia, Fed. Sts.	0	0	0	0
Moldova	53.22	38.48	-0.28	-14.74

Monaco	0	0	0	0
Mongolia	51.79	52.42	0.01	0.63
Montenegro	34.26	34.53	0.01	0.26
Morocco	23.65	24.05	0.02	0.4
Mozambique	64.98	64.88	0	-0.1
Myanmar	70.23	72.15	0.03	1.92
Namibia	38.96	42.09	0.08	3.13
Nepal	78.76	78.12	-0.01	-0.65
Netherlands	48.01	55.44	0.15	7.43
New Zealand	52.67	57.86	0.1	5.19
Nicaragua	34.9	42.59	0.22	7.69
Niger	33.05	37.81	0.14	4.76
Nigeria	40.43	44.35	0.1	3.92
Norway	56.23	59.4	0.06	3.17
Oman	17.95	23.23	0.29	5.28
Pakistan	12.83	20.17	0.57	7.35
Palau	0	0	0	0
Panama	35.58	44.1	0.24	8.52
Papua New Guinea	67.99	68.72	0.01	0.73
Paraguay	48.3	51.43	0.06	3.13
Peru	52.48	61.53	0.17	9.05
Philippines	44.76	46.13	0.03	1.36
Poland	41.91	42	0	0.09
Portugal	48.27	49.22	0.02	0.95
Qatar	39.11	47.43	0.21	8.32
Romania	52.28	45.56	-0.13	-6.72
Russian Federation	48.02	53.19	0.11	5.17
Rwanda	85.81	85.95	0	0.15
Samoa	0	0	0	0
San Marino	0	0	0	0
Sao Tome and Principe	0	0	0	0
Saudi Arabia	13.62	14.96	0.1	1.35
Senegal	56.25	57.24	0.02	0.98
Serbia	37.07	34.67	-0.06	-2.4
Seychelles	0	0	0	0
Sierra Leone	63.37	64.14	0.01	0.76
Singapore	48.95	54.28	0.11	5.33
Slovak Republic	44.36	43.57	-0.02	-0.79
Slovenia	47.7	48.83	0.02	1.13
Solomon Islands	50.43	51.2	0.02	0.77
Somalia	33.17	34.15	0.03	0.98

South Africa	33.93	32.89	-0.03	-1.04
South Sudan	0	0	0	0
Spain	29.34	40.4	0.38	11.06
Sri Lanka	30.97	32.72	0.06	1.75
St. Kitts and Nevis	0	0	0	0
St. Lucia	0	0	0	0
St. Vincent and the Grenadines	0	0	0	0
Sudan	22.4	24.21	0.08	1.81
Suriname	29.49	35.32	0.2	5.83
Swaziland	31.75	32.15	0.01	0.39
Sweden	54.05	55.18	0.02	1.13
Switzerland	55.52	57.95	0.04	2.44
Syrian Arab Republic	16.95	10.78	-0.36	-6.16
Tajikistan	52.16	52.25	0	0.08
Tanzania	82.15	84.94	0.03	2.78
Thailand	64.6	64.34	0	-0.26
Timor-Leste	34.89	25.45	-0.27	-9.44
Togo	68.58	74.4	0.08	5.82
Tonga	0	0	0	0
Trinidad and Tobago	37.95	48.86	0.29	10.91
Tunisia	19.03	20.74	0.09	1.71
Turkey	26.34	23.32	-0.11	-3.02
Turkmenistan	42.22	41.55	-0.02	-0.67
Tuvalu	0	0	0	0
Uganda	78.39	73.28	-0.07	-5.11
Ukraine	48.74	49.09	0.01	0.35
United Arab Emirates	30.23	39.23	0.3	9
United Kingdom	50.29	52.19	0.04	1.9
United States	55.25	53.87	-0.02	-1.37
Uruguay	44.5	48.86	0.1	4.36
Uzbekistan	41.88	42.38	0.01	0.5
Vanuatu	0	0	0	0
Venezuela, RB	39.75	45.78	0.15	6.04
Vietnam	71.5	70.81	-0.01	-0.69
Yemen, Rep.	13.26	15.27	0.15	2.01
Zambia	64.93	64.25	-0.01	-0.67
Zimbabwe	66.28	79	0.19	12.72
	39.89	**41.94**	**0.05**	**2.05**

(The World Bank Group, 2016)

The fifty-third through the fifty-sixth measurements calculated the annual employment to population ratio averages, percentage of change, and shift for males who were fifteen years or older between the 1993 to 2003 time period and the 2004 and 2014 time period for 193 nations in the world with the exception of Nauru and the Vatican City State (Nations Online, 2016).

Country Name	1993-2003 Average	2004-2014 Average	% of Change	Male Employment Shift
Afghanistan	75.62	73.82	-0.02	-1.8
Albania	63.61	57.45	-0.10	-6.16
Algeria	58.73	64.21	0.09	5.48
Andorra	0.00	0.00	0.00	0
Angola	70.37	71.78	0.02	1.41
Antigua and Barbuda	0.00	0.00	0.00	0
Argentina	64.50	69.84	0.08	5.34
Armenia	58.89	57.20	-0.03	-1.69
Australia	67.01	68.57	0.02	1.56
Austria	66.72	64.76	-0.03	-1.95
Azerbaijan	66.30	64.95	-0.02	-1.35
Bahamas, The	70.92	69.89	-0.01	-1.03
Bahrain	83.59	82.95	-0.01	-0.64
Bangladesh	83.83	81.27	-0.03	-2.55
Barbados	66.75	69.80	0.05	3.05
Belarus	62.09	57.62	-0.07	-4.47
Belgium	56.56	55.69	-0.02	-0.87
Belize	76.05	75.78	0.00	-0.26
Benin	82.66	77.61	-0.06	-5.05
Bhutan	77.54	74.89	-0.03	-2.65
Bolivia	78.81	78.69	0.00	-0.12
Bosnia and Herzegovina	43.45	42.45	-0.02	-0.99
Botswana	64.41	68.10	0.06	3.69
Brazil	77.62	76.60	-0.01	-1.02
Brunei Darussalam	77.10	73.92	-0.04	-3.18
Bulgaria	47.98	52.96	0.10	4.98
Burkina Faso	87.55	86.79	-0.01	-0.75
Burundi	79.45	76.35	-0.04	-3.1
Cambodia	82.23	85.70	0.04	3.47
Cameroon	72.72	73.75	0.01	1.03
Canada	65.93	66.50	0.01	0.57
Cabo Verde	77.35	76.66	-0.01	-0.69

Central African Republic	80.39	79.58	-0.01	-0.81
Chad	74.63	74.07	-0.01	-0.55
Chile	70.31	69.06	-0.02	-1.25
China	79.25	74.69	-0.06	-4.56
Colombia	71.85	72.53	0.01	0.67
Congo, Dem. Rep.	68.98	68.14	-0.01	-0.85
Congo, Rep.	67.25	67.97	0.01	0.73
Costa Rica	78.31	75.25	-0.04	-3.05
Cote d'Ivoire	79.55	78.37	-0.01	-1.18
Croatia	56.66	52.73	-0.07	-3.94
Cuba	67.50	67.45	0.00	-0.05
Curacao	0.00	0.00	0.00	0
Cyprus	68.00	66.45	-0.02	-1.55
Czech Republic	66.87	64.41	-0.04	-2.46
Denmark	68.45	65.65	-0.04	-2.8
Djibouti	0.00	0.00	0.00	0
Dominica	0.00	0.00	0.00	0
Dominican Republic	72.73	71.55	-0.02	-1.18
Ecuador	80.04	80.04	0.00	0
Egypt, Arab Rep.	68.43	69.31	0.01	0.88
El Salvador	73.04	72.32	-0.01	-0.72
Equatorial Guinea	87.04	86.15	-0.01	-0.89
Eritrea	84.84	83.43	-0.02	-1.41
Estonia	61.63	61.04	-0.01	-0.59
Ethiopia	87.17	87.45	0.00	0.27
Fiji	73.43	68.09	-0.07	-5.34
Finland	58.70	59.85	0.02	1.15
France	57.11	56.59	-0.01	-0.52
Gabon	55.70	55.06	-0.01	-0.64
Gambia, The	78.57	77.77	-0.01	-0.8
Georgia	65.00	62.35	-0.04	-2.65
Germany	62.95	61.25	-0.03	-1.7
Ghana	69.09	68.71	-0.01	-0.38
Greece	61.03	56.59	-0.07	-4.44
Grenada	0.00	0.00	0.00	0
Guatemala	84.46	85.69	0.01	1.23
Guinea	76.48	76.69	0.00	0.21
Guinea-Bissau	73.49	73.42	0.00	-0.07
Guyana	73.63	73.18	-0.01	-0.45
Haiti	65.83	65.80	0.00	-0.03
Honduras	84.16	80.43	-0.04	-3.74
Hungary	53.00	53.69	0.01	0.69
Iceland	78.36	75.10	-0.04	-3.26

India	80.12	78.42	-0.02	-1.7
Indonesia	79.17	78.65	-0.01	-0.53
Iran, Islamic Rep.	66.63	65.09	-0.02	-1.54
Iraq	57.60	58.66	0.02	1.06
Ireland	63.61	62.74	-0.01	-0.87
Israel	56.46	59.24	0.05	2.77
Italy	56.65	55.60	-0.02	-1.05
Jamaica	70.85	67.19	-0.05	-3.65
Japan	73.68	68.71	-0.07	-4.97
Jordan	59.43	60.10	0.01	0.67
Kazakhstan	69.77	72.47	0.04	2.7
Kenya	68.35	65.50	-0.04	-2.85
Kiribati	0.00	0.00	0.00	0
Korea, Dem. People's Rep.	84.01	80.68	-0.04	-3.33
Korea, Rep.	71.15	69.69	-0.02	-1.45
Kosovo	0.00	0.00	0.00	0
Kuwait	81.44	80.36	-0.01	-1.07
Kyrgyz Republic	68.15	71.89	0.05	3.74
Lao PDR	79.46	77.76	-0.02	-1.7
Latvia	59.00	58.92	0.00	-0.08
Lebanon	65.06	66.34	0.02	1.27
Lesotho	59.60	56.37	-0.05	-3.23
Liberia	60.13	61.16	0.02	1.04
Libya	61.73	63.90	0.04	2.17
Liechtenstein	0.00	0.00	0.00	0
Lithuania	58.15	56.91	-0.02	-1.24
Luxembourg	64.56	61.86	-0.04	-2.7
Macedonia, FYR	44.95	44.88	0.00	-0.06
Madagascar	87.02	87.72	0.01	0.7
Malawi	75.69	77.32	0.02	1.63
Malaysia	77.72	73.75	-0.05	-3.96
Maldives	68.06	70.72	0.04	2.65
Mali	61.47	72.20	0.17	10.73
Malta	68.61	63.17	-0.08	-5.44
Marshall Islands	0.00	0.00	0.00	0
Mauritania	52.37	53.66	0.02	1.29
Mauritius	75.41	71.40	-0.05	-4.01
Mexico	80.38	77.07	-0.04	-3.31
Micronesia, Fed. Sts.	0.00	0.00	0.00	0
Moldova	60.61	43.53	-0.28	-17.08
Monaco	0.00	0.00	0.00	0
Mongolia	61.36	62.99	0.03	1.63

Montenegro	49.10	48.19	-0.02	-0.91
Morocco	68.92	69.56	0.01	0.65
Mozambique	64.91	66.55	0.03	1.65
Myanmar	77.32	79.32	0.03	2
Namibia	52.59	52.91	0.01	0.32
Nepal	87.56	85.59	-0.02	-1.97
Netherlands	68.85	68.72	0.00	-0.13
New Zealand	68.59	70.85	0.03	2.26
Nicaragua	78.66	75.28	-0.04	-3.38
Niger	84.79	85.37	0.01	0.58
Nigeria	63.42	58.06	-0.08	-5.35
Norway	67.87	67.47	-0.01	-0.4
Oman	74.79	74.43	0.00	-0.36
Pakistan	79.46	79.55	0.00	0.09
Palau	0.00	0.00	0.00	0
Panama	72.81	77.42	0.06	4.61
Papua New Guinea	70.86	72.61	0.02	1.75
Paraguay	83.30	81.37	-0.02	-1.93
Peru	77.30	79.91	0.03	2.61
Philippines	75.52	73.51	-0.03	-2.01
Poland	56.06	56.84	0.01	0.77
Portugal	65.98	61.54	-0.07	-4.45
Qatar	93.29	94.87	0.02	1.58
Romania	64.82	59.10	-0.09	-5.72
Russian Federation	61.57	65.53	0.06	3.95
Rwanda	85.66	84.18	-0.02	-1.48
Samoa	0.00	0.00	0.00	0
San Marino	0.00	0.00	0.00	0
Sao Tome and Principe	0.00	0.00	0.00	0
Saudi Arabia	72.53	72.66	0.00	0.14
Senegal	82.05	81.44	-0.01	-0.61
Serbia	57.07	51.53	-0.10	-5.55
Seychelles	0.00	0.00	0.00	0
Sierra Leone	60.64	65.06	0.07	4.43
Singapore	76.45	74.81	-0.02	-1.64
Slovak Republic	58.51	59.48	0.02	0.97
Slovenia	59.72	60.74	0.02	1.02
Solomon Islands	75.08	76.45	0.02	1.37
Somalia	72.38	71.01	-0.02	-1.37
South Africa	51.41	48.27	-0.06	-3.14
South Sudan	0.00	0.00	0.00	0
Spain	56.78	56.87	0.00	0.09
Sri Lanka	71.14	73.24	0.03	2.1

St. Kitts and Nevis	0.00	0.00	0.00	0
St. Lucia	0.00	0.00	0.00	0
St. Vincent and the Grenadines	0.00	0.00	0.00	0
Sudan	65.69	66.80	0.02	1.11
Suriname	61.02	64.60	0.06	3.58
Swaziland	57.45	56.31	-0.02	-1.14
Sweden	61.64	62.79	0.02	1.15
Switzerland	75.94	72.51	-0.05	-3.43
Syrian Arab Republic	75.82	68.85	-0.09	-6.96
Tajikistan	65.52	66.54	0.02	1.02
Tanzania	88.06	88.50	0.00	0.44
Thailand	80.30	80.17	0.00	-0.13
Timor-Leste	71.95	54.18	-0.25	-17.76
Togo	76.61	75.51	-0.01	-1.1
Tonga	0.00	0.00	0.00	0
Trinidad and Tobago	66.57	72.52	0.09	5.95
Tunisia	62.26	60.85	-0.02	-1.41
Turkey	68.50	63.22	-0.08	-5.28
Turkmenistan	65.86	67.54	0.03	1.67
Tuvalu	0.00	0.00	0.00	0
Uganda	80.46	77.28	-0.04	-3.18
Ukraine	59.78	60.31	0.01	0.53
United Arab Emirates	90.19	88.25	-0.02	-1.95
United Kingdom	64.85	64.29	-0.01	-0.55
United States	69.80	65.54	-0.06	-4.26
Uruguay	71.20	71.97	0.01	0.77
Uzbekistan	64.33	66.12	0.03	1.79
Vanuatu	0.00	0.00	0.00	0
Venezuela, RB	73.34	73.39	0.00	0.05
Vietnam	81.24	80.03	-0.01	-1.21
Yemen, Rep.	66.47	65.04	-0.02	-1.44
Zambia	70.56	72.08	0.02	1.52
Zimbabwe	76.51	84.84	0.11	8.33
61.23	**60.63**	**-0.01**	**-0.61**

(The World Bank Group, 2016)

Discussion

The first through the fourth measurements calculated the annual primary completion rate averages, percentage of change, and shift for females that were twenty-five years or older between the 1993 to 2003 time period and the 2004 and 2014 time period for 193 nations in the world with the exception of Nauru and the Vatican City State (Nations Online, 2016).

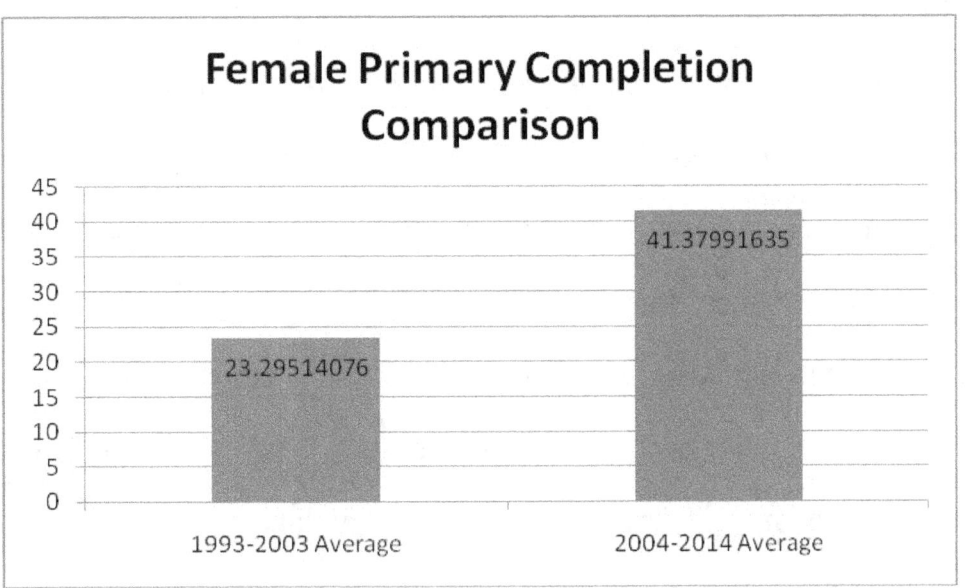

There was infrequent reporting by all of the 193 nations analyzed for both the 1993 to 2003 time period and the 2004 to 2014 time period. There was more consistent reporting in the 2004 to 2014 time period, but there were still many nations measured that failed to report statistics regarding the annual primary completion rate data for females to the World Bank Group. From the data obtained, it can be concluded that the annual primary completion rate for females increased by 77% between the 1993 to 2003 time period and the 2004 to 2014 time period. There was an annual primary completion rate for females positive shift of 18.08 between the 1993 to 2003 time period and the 2004 to 2014 time period, but the results of the measurement would have been even more accurate with better annual reporting by nations. Primary education for both sexes has been a problem throughout the world for centuries, and it persists today in developing countries despite some progress made over the last couple of decades (UNESCO, 2009). Over the last decade, many developing countries have seen female enrollment in primary education schools increase at a faster rate than males, which has helped closed the gender gap in these nations. There has been a general upward trend in developing nations over the last three decades in enrollment in primary schools for both sexes, and the most dramatic improvement has been seen in sub-Saharan Africa, Asia, and the Middle East. There have been declines reported in the number of students enrolled in primary schools in nations in Central Asia and Eastern Europe, which has been seen for both sexes despite declining numbers of school-aged children in these regions. North America and Western Europe have shown steady ratios of both male and female students enrolled in primary schools for decades. The lowest enrollment rates in the world for female primary students is in the Middle East, and the states with the largest gender gaps favoring males are in both sub-Saharan Africa and the Middle East. School enrollment at all levels of education has increased over the last three decades, and nearly 75% of the world's children live in nations that provide universal primary education to both sexes. Drop-out rates of school-aged children have decreased as well, and youth literacy rates are higher than adult populations throughout the world. The goal of reaching gender parity has been reached in almost 75% of the nations throughout the world, and female enrollment rates in all levels of education continue to increase faster than those of males. Female children do experience discrimination in relation to access to primary education in some countries, and the gender parity reached in many nations in primary and secondary schooling is not seen at the tertiary level of education. Despite increased access to education for females in developing nations throughout the world, a higher education level does not translate into gender parity for employment opportunities. Females are still facing large amounts of discrimination in labor markets throughout the world, and they often end up working in jobs that do not utilize any of the educational skills that they have gained from schooling. Therefore, increased educational opportunities have not translated to increased female empowerment in all nations as it relates to employment and economics.

The fifth through the eighth measurements calculated the annual primary completion rate averages, percentage of change, and shift for females that were twenty-five years or older between the 2007 to 2010 time period and the 2011 to 2014 time period for nations that reported annual primary completion rate data every year from 2007 to 2014 for 193 nations in the world with the exception of Nauru and the Vatican City State (Nations Online, 2016).

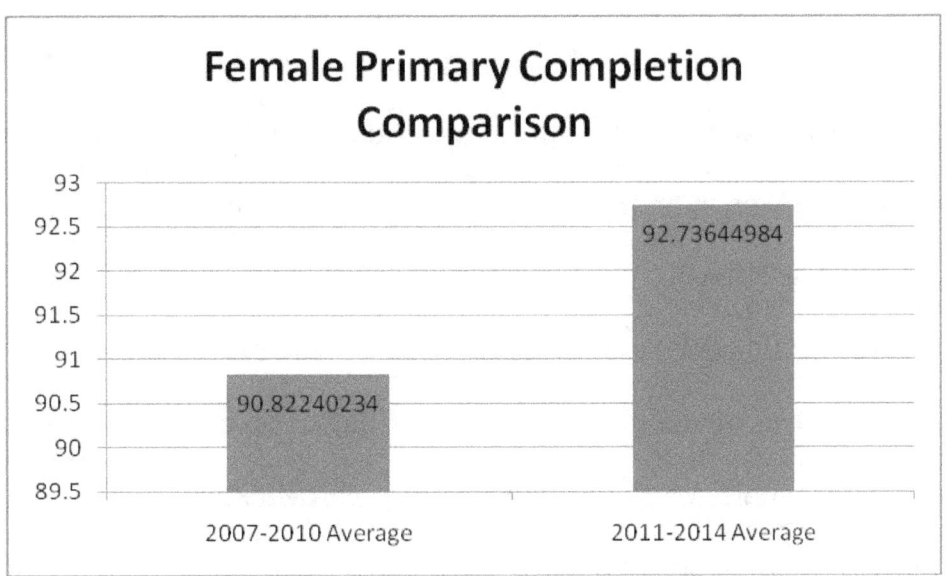

There were sixteen nations out of 193 that reported annual primary completion rate for females' data every year from 2007 to 2014. The percentage of change for annual primary completion rate for females between the 2007 to 2010 time period and the 2011 to 2014 time period for all nations measured was 2%, and the annual primary completion rate for females between the 2007 to 2010 time period and the 2011 to 2014 time period for all nations measured showed a positive shift of 1.91 This data shows a general trend of increased primary school attendance for the sixteen nations analyzed in accordance with other measurements in this study and the literature cited in this research, which is positive and shows a move toward gender parity within these nations. Since the beginning of the twenty-first century, there has been considerable progress made in disparities between male and female enrollment rates in primary education throughout the world (UNESCO, 2015). Since 1999, gender disparity has been reduced from ninety-two to ninety-seven females enrolled for every 100 males enrolled, which shows a substantial reduction but not an elimination of the gender gap. The regions that showed the strongest progress in achieving gender parity were in Asia, specifically in the Islamic Republic of Iran, India, Sri Lanka, and Bhutan. Asia, however, has shown to have one of the largest variations in annual female primary enrollment rates with Nepal reversing the gender gap in 2012 and Afghanistan with only seventy-two females enrolled in primary schools for every 100 males. Throughout the world, poor children, especially females, have the greatest risk of being out of schools. At the beginning of the twenty-first century, sub-Saharan Africa was the region with the highest rate of children that have never attended school, and the highest proportion of the population to have never attended schools within this region were impoverished female children. There are presently nearly 60 million children that are at primary school-age that are not enrolled in school, which has decreased from 105 million since the beginning of the twenty-first century. Sub-Saharan Africa, however, showed an increase of primary age school children out of school from 40% to 50% since the beginning of the twenty-first century. Out-of-school children fall into three categories: children who will eventually attend school, children who will never attend school, and children who have enrolled in school but dropped out. Research shows that despite females being less likely to enroll in primary school than males throughout the world they are more likely to continue attending into upper grades than males. There has been progress in the twenty-first century in increasing female primary school enrollment rates, which has resulted from government legislation, advocacy, and community mobilization. These legislative and social advancements have been reinforced with a greater allocation of resource implementation at the school, district, and national level. Female students at all levels still face barriers, such as: violence, discrimination, negative schooling experiences, and poor gender relations. In societies in which gender parity has been reached in education, females are still at a disadvantage in political, economic, and civic life. Education should help societies address gender biases and lead to the empowerment of both sexes, and allow individuals in societies to challenge traditional norms as it pertains to gender and position individuals to make improved and informed decisions about their lives for better futures.

The ninth through the twelfth measurements calculated the annual primary completion rate averages, percentage of change, and shift for males that were twenty-five years or older between the 1993 to 2003 time period and the 2004 and 2014 time period for 193 nations in the world with the exception of Nauru and the Vatican City State (Nations Online, 2016).

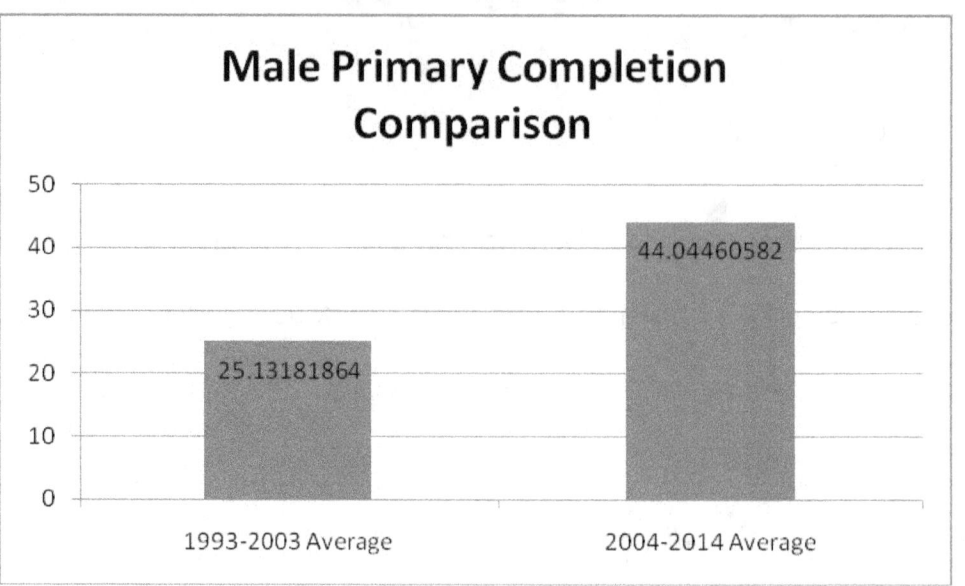

There was sporadic reporting by all of the 193 nations analyzed for both the 1993 to 2003 time period and the 2004 to 2014 time period. There was more consistent reporting in the 2004 to 2014 time period, but there were still many nations measured that failed to report statistics regarding the annual primary completion rate data for males to the World Bank Group. From the data obtained, it can be concluded that the annual primary completion rate for males increased by 75% between the 1993 to 2003 time period and the 2004 to 2014 time period. There was an annual primary completion rate for males positive shift of 18.91 between the 1993 to 2003 time period and the 2004 to 2014 time period, but the results of the measurement would have been even more accurate with better annual reporting by nations. The goal of universal primary education for all children set by the United Nations has not presently been achieved, but there has been continued enrollment in primary schools throughout the world since the beginning of the twenty-first century (UN Department of Public Education, 2010). Over the last decade, primary enrollment has increased by 20% in sub-Saharan Africa, 10% in Northern Africa, and by nearly 10% in Asia. The UN's goal of reaching universal primary education in which all males and females complete a full course of elementary schooling by 2015 was not met, and there are presently almost 70 million school-age children that are not attending school throughout the world. There are currently 31 million children who are not attending primary school in sub-Saharan African, and about 20 million children not attending primary school in Asia. Throughout the developing world dropout rates remain high, and over 30% of children that have enrolled in primary school and attended some class end up dropping out before completing their primary education in sub-Saharan Africa. Abolishing school fees have helped increase attendance rates in primary schools throughout the world, especially in developing countries. This has led to an increase in the number of students, and the needs of these students have not been properly met in all nations. There is presently a shortage of enough qualified teachers, classrooms, and resources in most schools throughout the developing world. There has been some progress in resource allocation, but most of it has been temporary. This includes recruiting retirees and volunteers to instruct primary school students, and the development of temporary classrooms and the acquiring of teaching materials to ensure that students have access to schooling. Other methods that have helped to make primary educational progress throughout the world are mobile schools and bilingual educational programs that deliver schooling in indigenous languages. There has been a lot of progress made throughout the world in an attempt to achieve UPE, but there is a lot of work that needs to be done to reach this goal. More school-age children are attending primary school throughout the world than ever before, but there are still many obstacles that must be overcome to reach the UN's goal. Nations need to enact legislation that enables children access to sustainable education systems with qualified teachers, permanent infrastructure, and adequate resources to maintain the progress that has already been made.

The thirteenth through the sixteenth measurements calculated the annual primary completion rate averages, percentage of change, and shift for males that were twenty-five years or older between the 2007 to 2010 time period and the 2011 to 2014 time period for nations that reported annual primary completion rate data every year from 2007 to 2014 for 193 nations in the world with the exception of Nauru and the Vatican City State (Nations Online, 2016).

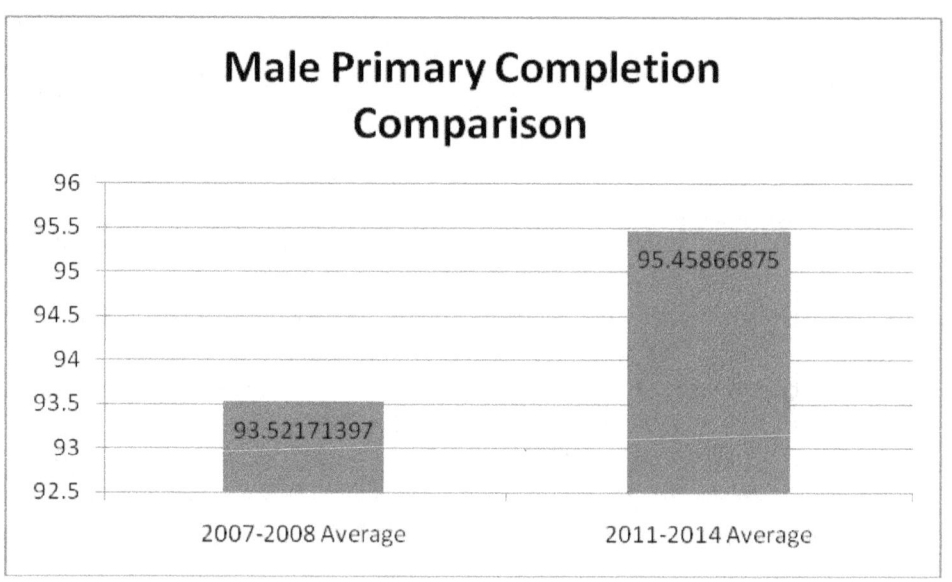

There were sixteen nations out of 193 that reported annual primary completion rate for males' data every year from 2007 to 2014. The percentage of change for annual primary completion rate for males between the 2007 to 2010 time period and the 2011 to 2014 time period for all nations measured was 1.2%, and the annual primary completion rate for males between the 2007 to 2010 time period and the 2011 to 2014 time period for all nations measured showed a positive shift of 1.13. This data shows a general trend of increased primary school attendance in the sixteen nations analyzed in accordance with other measurements in this study and the literature cited in this research, which is positive and shows a move toward improved access and education quality for primary school students throughout the world. There are over 100 million children of primary school-age that are not in schools throughout the world, which is predominantly comprised of children in the poorest nations in Africa and Asia (Filmer, 2005). Policy interventions that include increasing school availability, the provision of cash subsidies for school participation, and promoting school quality have all had a beneficial effect on school enrollment rates. In most nations, policies that have lowered the distance to school for primary school-age children has resulted in increased enrollment rates, and the construction of schools is considered to be a much more straightforward process than ensuring the quality of schooling according to analysts Unfortunately, the association between building a physical school and lowering the distance of commuting for children has been shown not to increase and sustain enrollment of primary school-age children contrary to the political benefits for policymakers because it results in something tangible within communities. Research has shown that construction of schools in developing countries in conjunction with improving the quality of educational delivery can increase primary school enrollment at a higher rate. Therefore, policymakers must consider both school availability and the quality of education to ensure educational progress in their nations as it pertains to increased enrollment rates of primary school-age children.

The seventeenth through the twentieth measurements calculated the annual lower secondary completion rate averages, percentage of change, and shift for females that were twenty-five years or older between the 1993 to 2003 time period and the 2004 and 2014 time period for 193 nations in the world with the exception of Nauru and the Vatican City State (Nations Online, 2016).

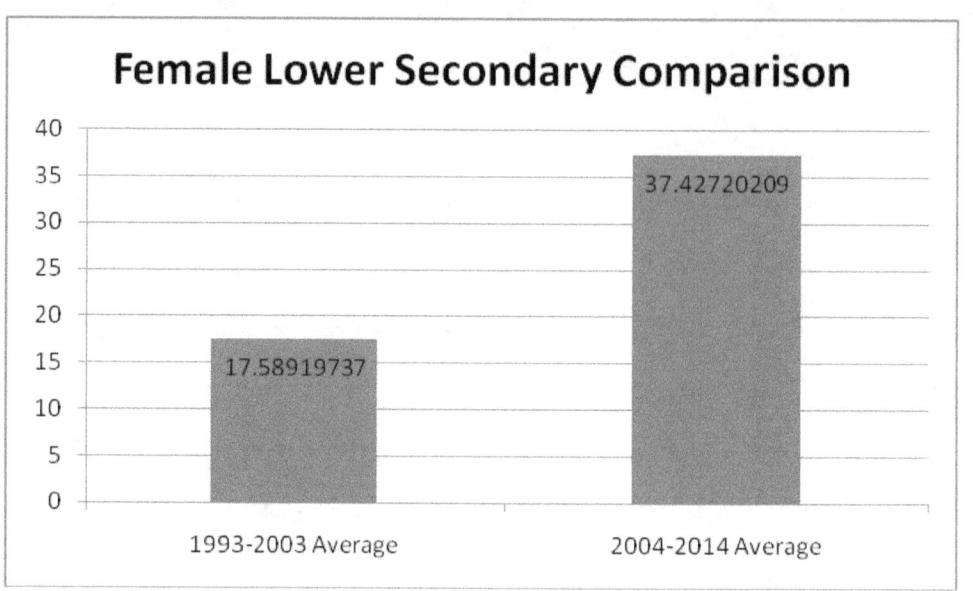

There was inconsistent reporting by all of the 193 nations analyzed for both the 1993 to 2003 time period and the 2004 to 2014 time period. There was more consistent reporting in the 2004 to 2014 time period, but there were still many nations measured that failed to report statistics regarding the annual lower secondary completion rate data for females to the World Bank Group. From the data obtained, it can be concluded that the annual lower secondary completion rate for females increased by 113% between the 1993 to 2003 time period and the 2004 to 2014 time period. There was an annual lower secondary completion rate for females positive shift of 19.84 between the 1993 to 2003 time period and the 2004 to 2014 time period, but the results of the measurement would have been even more accurate with better annual reporting by nations. There have been substantial gains in the twenty-first century in increasing school enrollment throughout the world, but the goal of universal primary and secondary education for all adolescents has not been met (UNICEF, 2015). The rate of out-of-school adolescents has not dropped since 2007, and there are presently over 60 million adolescents of lower secondary school-age who are not enrolled in schools throughout the world. The focus of universal education has been mainly on primary schooling, but lower secondary education has been recognized as essential for assisting adolescents in developing a foundation for a decent and healthy life in conjunction with helping them to develop the necessary skills to be productive in societies and national workforces. Of the more than 60 million adolescents not enrolled in lower secondary education, more than 40% of these adolescents live in sub-Saharan Africa or Asia. Although the statistics for primary school-age children and lower secondary school-age adolescents are similar, there are 650 million primary school-age children in the world and 374 million lower secondary school-age adolescents in the world. Therefore, lower secondary school-age adolescents are 200% more likely not to be enrolled in lower secondary schooling than primary school-age children throughout the world. There are a number of social and economic factors that contribute to the lack of enrollment of lower secondary school-age adolescents, which include family pressure to find employment to provide income and being placed in remedial courses for lack of attendance in primary school. In many nations throughout the world, lower secondary school-age adolescents between the ages of 12 and 15 often have no option but to work. Gender disparities for lower secondary school-age children are highest in sub-Saharan Africa, North Africa, and the Middle East, and these gender gaps in lower secondary education have been found to increase in regions in conjunction with decreased enrollment rates in lower secondary schooling. Gender disparity has decreased since the beginning of the twenty-first century as it pertains to lower secondary education, but females are still more likely than males in lower secondary schools to face consistent barriers to te educational process in many nations throughout the world. In developing nations throughout the world, cultural barriers persist surrounding gender norms that prevent female adolescents from attending lower secondary schools. These usually work in combination with one another, and the result is that young female adolescents do not enroll in lower secondary schools with the frequency of males in accordance with local laws. The gender norms and social situations that act as barriers include female genital mutilation, child marriage, poverty, child labor, ethnicity, and lack of family. These problems persist because of cultural and economic reasons, and the result is that laws surrounding cultural practices as it pertains to gender and compulsory education regulations are rarely enforced throughout the world, especially in developing countries. Education systems in place at the national level reflect environments within states, and they ultimately determine whether lower secondary school-age adolescents are enrolled in school or not. Legislation that has established compulsory education for lower secondary school-age adolescents can only be successful when it is matched by initiatives to address wider disadvantages within societies associated with poverty, gender, ethnicity, language, and residence.

The twenty-first through the twenty-fourth measurements calculated the annual lower secondary completion rate averages, percentage of change, and shift for females that were twenty-five years or older between the 2009 to 2011 time period and the 2012 to 2014 time period for nations that reported annual lower secondary completion rate data every year from 2009 to 2014 for 193 nations in the world with the exception of Nauru and the Vatican City State (Nations Online, 2016).

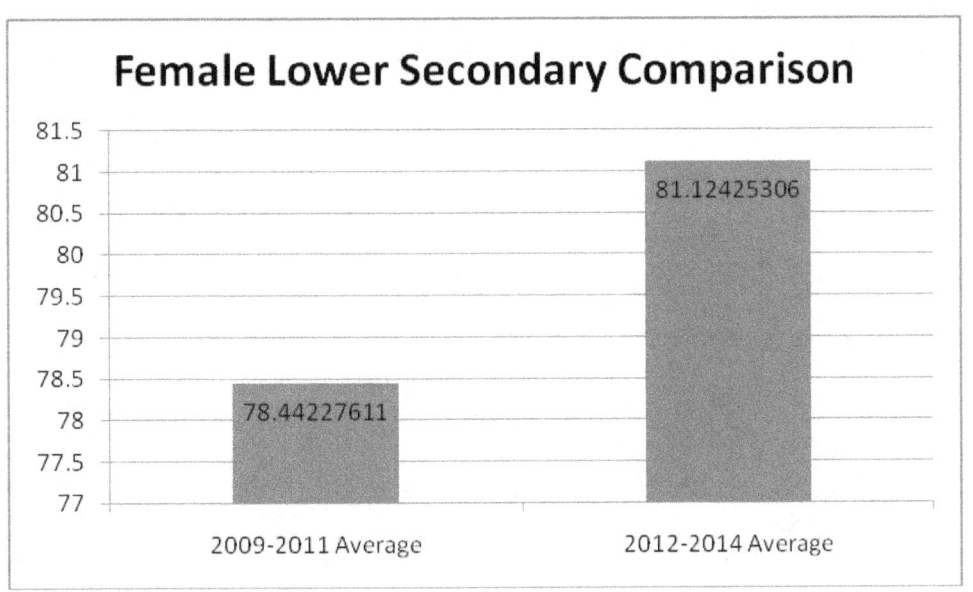

Female Lower Secondary Comparison

81.12425306 — 2012-2014 Average

78.44227611 — 2009-2011 Average

There were twenty-four nations out of 193 that reported annual lower secondary completion rate for females' data every year from 2009 to 2014. The percentage of change for annual lower secondary completion rate for females between the 2009 to 2011 time period and the 2012 to 2014 time period for all nations measured was 3%, and the annual lower secondary completion rate for females between the 2009 to 2010 time period and the 2011 to 2014 time period for all nations measured showed a positive shift of 2.68. This data shows a general trend of increased lower secondary school attendance for the twenty-fourth aforementioned nations in accordance with other measurements in this study and the literature cited in this research, which is positive and shows a move toward improved access and education quality for lower secondary school students throughout the world. Countries throughout the world have committed themselves to achieving universal education for both sexes, and most nations include both lower and upper secondary schooling in their national targets for universal education (UNICEF, 2016). Throughout the world, 83% of lower secondary school-age adolescents are enrolled in schools, but this number drops to 70% in developing countries in which lower secondary school-age adolescents face the largest social and economic challenges. At the beginning of the twenty-first century, there were 97 million lower secondary school-age adolescents not enrolled in schools, but this number has decreased to 65 million today. Unfortunately, progress in decreasing the number of lower secondary school-age adolescents who are not enrolled in school has not continued to decrease at the same rate seen at the beginning of the century, and the statistical evidence has remained the same since 2007 or over the last decade. Barriers to lower secondary enrollment for adolescents between the ages of twelve and fifteen are similar to those faced by primary school-age children. The cost of lower secondary schooling, however, is higher than primary schooling in most nations, and these educational institutions are generally further from students' homes and require transportation. Adolescents are generally pressured by their families because of financial circumstances to work, so lower secondary schooling is generally considered to be for a privileged fraction of the population in many countries throughout the world. This results in millions of adolescents entering the work force in many regions throughout the world without the necessary academic and life skills to be successful as adults. In sub-Saharan Africa, less than 50% of lower secondary school-age adolescents are enrolled in school, and less than 20% of lower secondary school-age adolescents are enrolled in schools in Angola, the Central African Republic, and Niger. Less than 50% of nations throughout the world have reach gender parity for lower secondary school enrollment, and the largest gender gaps in the world are seen in West and Central Africa in which 79 females are enrolled in lower secondary schools for every 100 males. Despite some progress in the world toward universal primary and secondary education, there are a large number of students throughout the world who are attending schools but who have failed to master basic reading and numeracy skills. Failure in lower secondary school by both sexes is attributed to entering primary schools late and erratic attendance to schooling, which leads to high dropout rates for both sexes in both lower and upper secondary schools.

The twenty-fifth through the twenty-eighth measurements calculated the annual lower secondary completion rate averages, percentage of change, and shift for males that were twenty-five years or older between the 1993 to 2003 time period and the 2004 and 2014 time period for 193 nations in the world with the exception of Nauru and the Vatican City State (Nations Online, 2016).

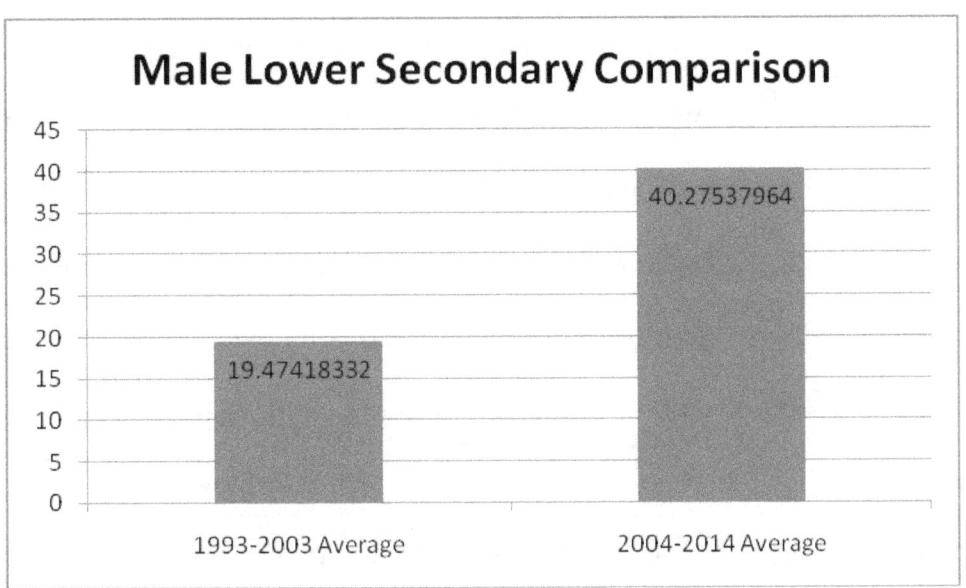

There was irregular reporting by all of the 193 nations analyzed for both the 1993 to 2003 time period and the 2004 to 2014 time period. There was more consistent reporting in the 2004 to 2014 time period, but there were still many nations measured that failed to report statistics regarding the annual lower secondary completion rate data for males to the World Bank Group. From the data obtained, it can be concluded that the annual lower secondary completion rate for males increased by 107% between the 1993 to 2003 time period and the 2004 to 2014 time period. There was an annual lower secondary completion rate for males positive shift of 20.80 between the 1993 to 2003 time period and the 2004 to 2014 time period, but the results of the measurement would have been even more accurate with better annual reporting by nations. There is a clear trend throughout the world of increased enrollment rates in both primary and secondary schooling, but there are large inequalities in education attainment that persist throughout the world today (Utomo et al., 2014). In many developing nations, the majority of adolescents never complete secondary education despite the increasing demand for skilled laborers in modern economies. In developing nations, when children become adolescents, early exits from secondary school are being documented at increasing rates, and the transition is not made by many adolescents as a result of economic factors. Economic factors typically include affordable education and pressure to earn a living, which has a similar effect throughout the world on adolescents and results in a cycle of intergenerational dependence because young people's socio-economic trajectories are derailed early on. There has been a positive relationship established in multiple research studies between enrollment and completion of schooling leading to more successful transitions into adulthood. Secondary school enrollment is important in developing nations because it has been positively associated with an increase in the age of marriage and childbearing, and young females with higher levels of education have fewer children and invest more in their children following childbirth. Dropping out of secondary education has been shown to lead to intergenerational cycles of poverty, low education attainment throughout individuals lives, and poor social outcomes. For impoverished adolescents, their families cannot often afford school fees associated with registration, the cost of books, school supplies, uniforms, and transport. Adolescents from low-income backgrounds are often pressured by their families to work because the benefit from paid labor is more important to families survival needs than school attendance. The lack of educational attainment has a negative effect on adolescents long-term growth, and dropping out of school results in decreased cognitive skills and negative health outcomes. Although adolescents are typically pressured by their families to drop out of school to become child laborers, individuals without secondary education usually face a life of low-income labor, joblessness, and inactivity. In general, the cycle of poverty typically produces generations of individuals that have perceptions of low financial returns from education, and inactivity that results from a lack of education and labor opportunities is caused by views surrounding the cost of transportation in comparison to the potential economic returns from engaging in the educational process or low-income work. Although some secondary school dropouts do engage in child labor, there is some evidence that many of these individuals spend years inactive before returning to school or joining workforces. Inactivity has greater negative impact on secondary school-age children than child labor, and it has been associated with increased marriage rates and parenthood. Most females that drop out of secondary school do not work in formal settings, and the labor force participation of most females includes childcare, elderly care, and domestic work, especially in comparison to their male counterparts who have also dropped out of secondary schooling.

The twenty-ninth through the thirty-second measurements calculated the annual lower secondary completion rate averages, percentage of change, and shift for males that were twenty-five years or older between the 2009 to 2011 time period and the 2012 to 2014 time period for nations that reported annual lower secondary completion rate data every year from 2009 to 2014 for 193 nations in the world with the exception of Nauru and the Vatican City State (Nations Online, 2016).

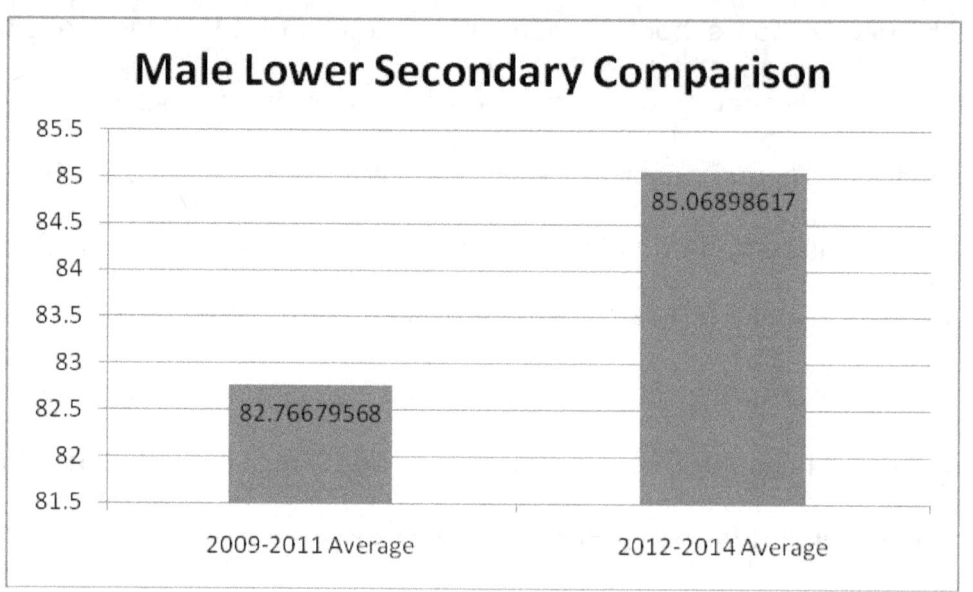

Male Lower Secondary Comparison

2009-2011 Average	82.76679568
2012-2014 Average	85.06898617

There were twenty-seven nations out of 193 that reported annual lower secondary completion rate for males' data every year from 2009 to 2014. The percentage of change for annual lower secondary completion rate for males between the 2009 to 2011 time period and the 2012 to 2014 time period for all nations measured was 3%, and the annual lower secondary completion rate for males between the 2009 to 2011 time period and the 2012 to 2014 time period for all nations measured showed a positive shift of 2.30. This data shows a general trend of increased lower secondary school attendance for the twenty-seven aforementioned nations in accordance with other measurements in this study and the literature cited in this research, which is positive and shows a move toward improved access and education quality for lower secondary school students throughout the world. Despite increased access and higher enrollment rates of lower secondary students throughout the world, attendance and achievement for males have been declining in many developing nations because of multiple factors (UNICEF, 2014). Many adolescents males are dropping out of schooling at earlier ages than previously seen, and there are fewer males continuing to higher education worldwide than in the past. This suggests that education systems are not meeting the basic requirements for young males in a manner previously seen, and this issue needs to be analyzed and addressed from both a community and a policy level. Within communities in developing nations, many young adolescent males are pressured to seek employment over schooling by their families and principal caregivers. There is also a perception in many of these communities that young males have an innate educational ability, and this is a reason that many adolescent males are unresponsive to traditional educational environments. Therefore, it is more beneficial for them and their families to support them in seeking gainful employment over educational opportunities. Many developing nations have limited educational resources, and the education that is provided for free and compulsory, according to national laws, is generally low-quality. Both male and female students are more likely to attend school if it is free and useful, but, despite this, adolescent male students are often ostracized by educators because of their sense of independence, which results in them being placed in the back of classrooms and receiving less attention from educators. This lack of attention coupled with male adolescents' sense of independence results in stereotypes by educators regarding their academic abilities, which leads to a cycle of poor performance and often results in increased dropout rates. This has also been attributed to a lower number of male educators at the secondary level in most developing nations in comparison to female educators, and it has been argued that this leads to a lack of positive male role models in young male adolescents' school environments. In many developing countries, there are gender stereotypes in which it is permitted to treat sexes differently, so young male adolescents typically fall into a stereotypical role where it is socially acceptable to have a negative relationship with schooling, which is reinforced in school and home environments. This results in the social acceptance and bias of young male adolescents having less opportunity to be successful in traditional educational environments, and it often leads to a gender bias within families in which they are given fewer resources for schooling by their primary caretakers than female adolescents. Educators need to address gender stereotypes for both sexes in school environments and tailor their educational delivery to meet all students' needs. Policymakers need to address circumstances faced at the economic level by impoverished students and the pressure adolescent males receive from primary caregivers to drop out of school to seek employment. Incentives need to be put in place to improve male adolescent attendance, and schools need to work to create learner-friendly environments for both sexes. Schools also need to incorporate more positive male role models in their environments, and they need to develop programs for both sexes that offer counseling and guidance.

The thirty-third through the thirty-sixth measurements calculated the annual upper secondary completion rate averages, percentage of change, and shift for females that were twenty-five years or older between the 1993 to 2003 time period and the 2004 and 2014 time period for 193 nations in the world with the exception of Nauru and the Vatican City State (Nations Online, 2016).

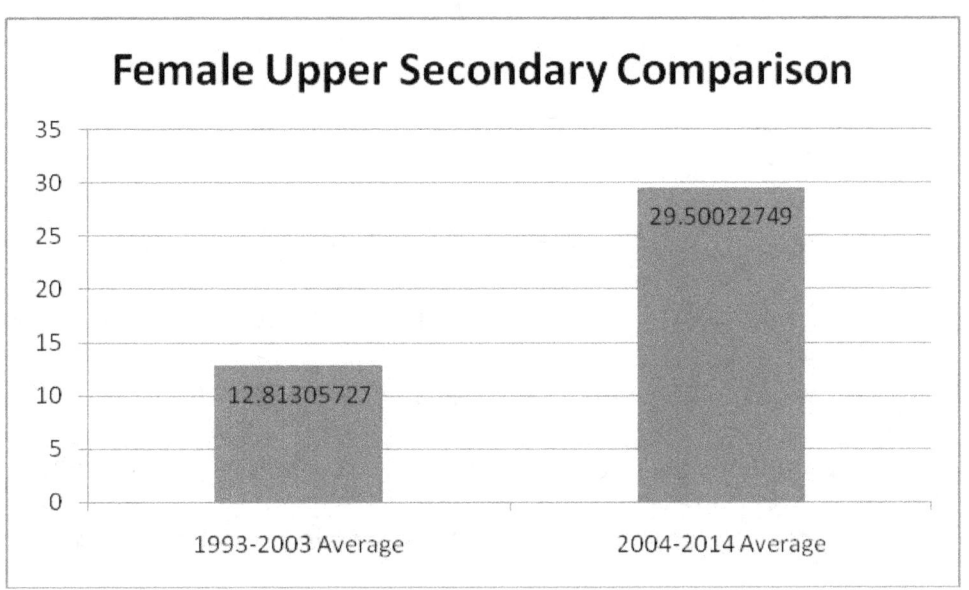

There was irregular reporting by all of the 193 nations analyzed for both the 1993 to 2003 time period and the 2004 to 2014 time period. There was more consistent reporting in the 2004 to 2014 time period, but there were still many nations measured that failed to report statistics regarding the annual upper secondary completion rate data for females to the World Bank Group. From the data obtained, it can be concluded that the annual upper secondary completion rate for females increased by 130% between the 1993 to 2003 time period and the 2004 to 2014 time period. There was an annual upper secondary completion rate for females positive shift of 16.69 between the 1993 to 2003 time period and the 2004 to 2014 time period, but the results of the measurement would have been even more accurate with better annual reporting by nations. Despite increased secondary enrollment and completion rates in countries throughout the world, nations must become more concerned about the quality of education provided and how this investment in human capital can positively effect economic and social growth (The World Bank Group, 2008). There is a direct relationship between government investment in education and economic return for nations, and, for most nations throughout the world, females represent a large percentage of the population that has been heavily invested in by national governments but under utilized in labor markets. The inclusion of more females in higher education and workforces can show favorable economic and social results within nations. This also has the indirect benefit of increasing labor force market competition, children's education, and renewing educational efforts at the policy level for incorporating both genders into schooling throughout nations. Gender equality has been achieved in some developing nations, with large gender gaps maintained by social norms, through education, which has resulted in females' entry into more lucrative jobs and raised wages. There is agreement, however, among most analysts that the positive effects of incorporating females into the educational process and higher-paying jobs are limited by cultural norms within nations, and females still face large amounts of discrimination at the educational and occupational level in most developing nations.

The thirty-seventh through fortieth measurements calculated the annual upper secondary completion rate averages, percentage of change, and shift for females that were twenty-five years or older between the 2009 to 2011 time period and the 2012 to 2014 time period for nations that reported annual upper secondary completion rate data every year from 2009 to 2014 for 193 nations in the world with the exception of Nauru and the Vatican City State (Nations Online, 2016).

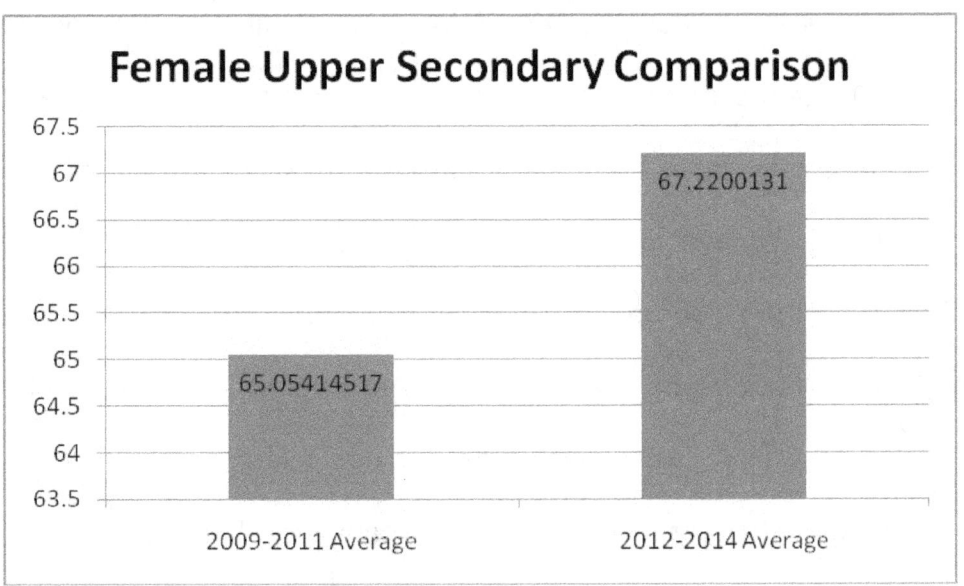

There were twenty-nine nations out of 193 that reported annual upper secondary completion rate for females' data every year from 2009 to 2014. The percentage of change for annual upper secondary completion rate for females between the 2009 to 2011 time period and the 2012 to 2014 time period for all nations measured was 3%, and the annual upper secondary completion rate for females between the 2009 to 2011 time period and the 2012 to 2014 time period for all nations measured showed a positive shift of 2.17. This data shows a general trend of increased upper secondary school attendance for the twenty-nine aforementioned nations in accordance with other measurements in this study and the literature cited in this research, which is positive and shows a move toward improved access and education quality for upper secondary school students throughout the world. Secondary education has become a more important policy and economic issue in nations throughout the world with globalization, and this will only increase in the future as females are increasingly utilized in labor markets throughout the world (UNESCO, 2005). In most nations throughout the world, primary education is state-funded, but governments are increasingly funding secondary education as well because the skills learned have become considered to be necessary for adolescents' basic education to assist them in being competitive within societies and labor markets. One of the main criticisms of secondary education worldwide is that it focuses too much on preparing the majority of students for tertiary education, which is not state-funded in every nation and not achievable by the majority of students in secondary schooling worldwide. Therefore, there are educators within secondary education systems throughout the world who believe that schooling at the secondary level should focus on both academic education and also education that allows students to gain the practical skills necessary for employment following the completion of secondary schooling. There are also educators who believe tracking students into educational streams in which they are divided into academic and vocational tracks is discriminatory. There are, however, social consequences to not tracking students in most nations in the world because students often feel inadequately trained upon graduation, employers have difficulty finding skilled graduates for the positions they are trying to fill, governments money is misallocated on educational programs that do not benefit the domestic economy, and there are increased numbers of secondary graduates who burden welfare systems with high unemployment rates. For secondary level students, there is a need for them to be educated and receive the tools that allow them effective ways of dealing with the economic pressure and cultural norms that they face in societies. Therefore, secondary education programs must maintain a suitable balance between academic, civic, and vocational training that allows adolescents to be competitive and empowered within their societies following graduation regardless of their gender.

The forty-first through the forty-fourth measurements calculated the annual upper secondary completion rate averages, percentage of change, and shift for males that were twenty-five years or older between the 1993 to 2003 time period and the 2004 and 2014 time period for 193 nations in the world with the exception of Nauru and the Vatican City State (Nations Online, 2016).

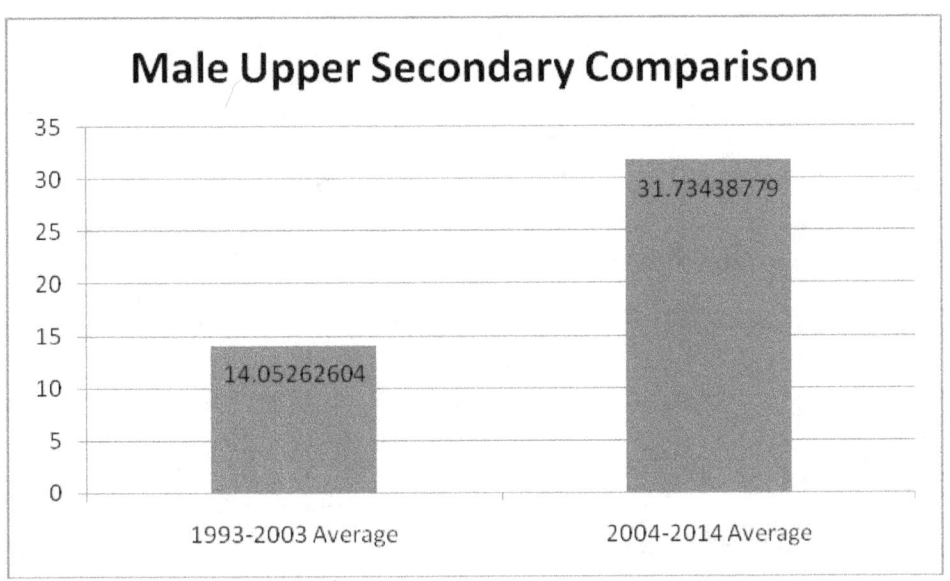

There was irregular reporting by all of the 193 nations analyzed for both the 1993 to 2003 time period and the 2004 to 2014 time period. There was more consistent reporting in the 2004 to 2014 time period, but there were still many nations measured that failed to report statistics regarding the annual upper secondary completion rate data for males to the World Bank Group. From the data obtained, it can be concluded that the annual upper secondary completion rate for males increased by 126% between the 1993 to 2003 time period and the 2004 to 2014 time period. There was an annual upper secondary completion rate for males positive shift of 17.68 between the 1993 to 2003 time period and the 2004 to 2014 time period, but the results of the measurement would have been even more accurate with better annual reporting by nations. The demand for secondary education is expanding worldwide as a result of globalization and with more children completing primary education (UNESCO, 2011). Throughout the world, primary education is no longer the most common exit point for males and females from schooling. Most countries throughout the world have made primary education compulsory, and more and more countries are making secondary education compulsory, too. The demand for secondary education will continue to increase as domestic economies have a greater need for more sophisticated workforces with relevant educational backgrounds and skill sets. The rapid expansion of secondary schools has resulted in increased investment by national governments in facilities, but this has come at the expense of quality, which has led to social, gender, and ethnic inequality at the domestic level. One concern throughout the world is the increased dropout rates of males who were formally enrolled in secondary education programs, which is highest in Latin America, Africa, Asia, and the Middle East. Females have a lower participation rate than males worldwide, but female enrollment has been increasing steadily since the beginning of the twenty-first century. Gender disparities still exist in many countries in sub-Saharan Africa, Asia, and the Middle East. Therefore, there are fewer females enrolling in secondary education worldwide, but they are more likely to complete secondary education in many regions throughout the world in comparison to males.

The forty-fifth through forty-eighth measurements calculated the annual upper secondary completion rate averages, percentage of change, and shift for males that were twenty-five years or older between the 2009 to 2011 time period and the 2012 to 2014 time period for nations that reported annual upper secondary completion rate data every year from 2009 to 2014 for 193 nations in the world with the exception of Nauru and the Vatican City State (Nations Online, 2016).

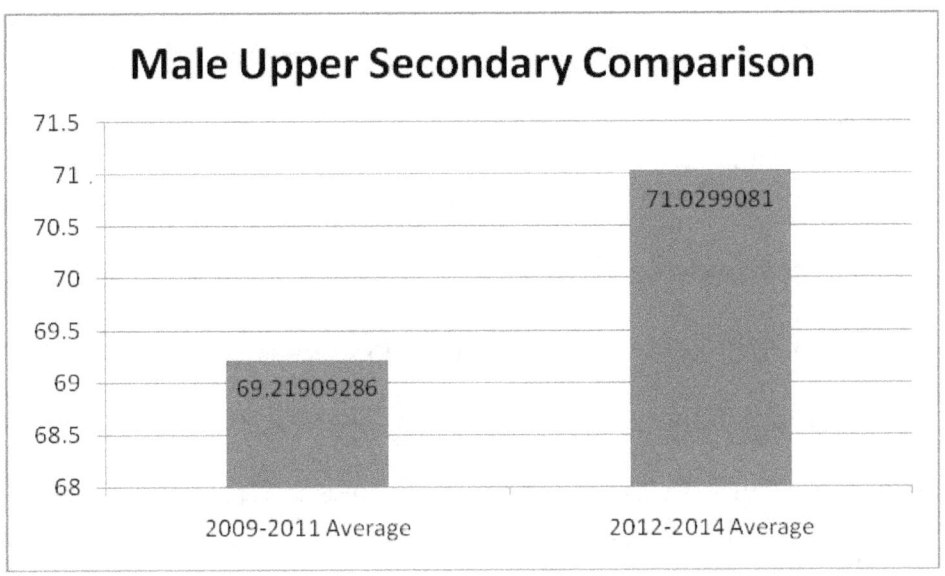

There were twenty-one nations out of 193 that reported annual upper secondary completion rate for males' data every year from 2009 to 2014. The percentage of change for annual upper secondary completion rate for males between the 2009 to 2011 time period and the 2012 to 2014 time period for all nations measured was 2.6%, and the annual upper secondary completion rate for males between the 2009 to 2011 time period and the 2012 to 2014 time period for all nations measured showed a positive shift of 1.81. This data shows a general trend of increased upper secondary school attendance for the twenty-one aforementioned nations in accordance with other measurements in this study and the literature cited in this research, which is positive and shows a move toward improved access and education quality for upper secondary school students throughout the world. There is an increasing need to focus on the transition between primary school and secondary school in all countries, but this transition has proved difficult in developing nations, especially for adolescent males (UNICEF, 2011). One of the main problems in developing countries is many young adolescents are not at grade-level when they enroll in secondary school, which causes them to have to repeat material taught in earlier grades to catch up to their peers and accounts for almost 40% of individuals who enroll in secondary schools in developing nations. Nearly 65% of individuals successfully transition from primary school to secondary school in developing nations, but they do not successfully advance to upper secondary education levels and complete schooling. For developing nations, about 50% of upper secondary school-age children are enrolled in secondary education programs, but the lack of enrollment is attributed to different factors related to gender. Adolescent females face forms of disadvantage and discrimination that are typically not encountered by males in developing nations, which include domestic labor, child marriage, social exclusion based on ethnicity, and pregnancy. Adolescent males face psychological challenges with traditional education in most developed nations, and they report lower satisfaction with the educational process and have a tendency to spend less time on academic activities than females. This has been attributed to peer influence, gender norms in societies, and family perceptions regarding education. There are around 150 million children subjected to child labor globally who typically work long hours and in hazardous conditions. Although child labor has decreased in the twenty-first century, there is substantial evidence that it is still prevalent, socially acceptable, and contributes to high dropout rates from schooling throughout the world, especially in developing countries.

The forty-ninth through the fifty-second measurements calculated the annual employment to population ratio averages, percentage of change, and shift for females who were fifteen years or older between the 1993 to 2003 time period and the 2004 and 2014 time period for 193 nations in the world with the exception of Nauru and the Vatican City State (Nations Online, 2016).

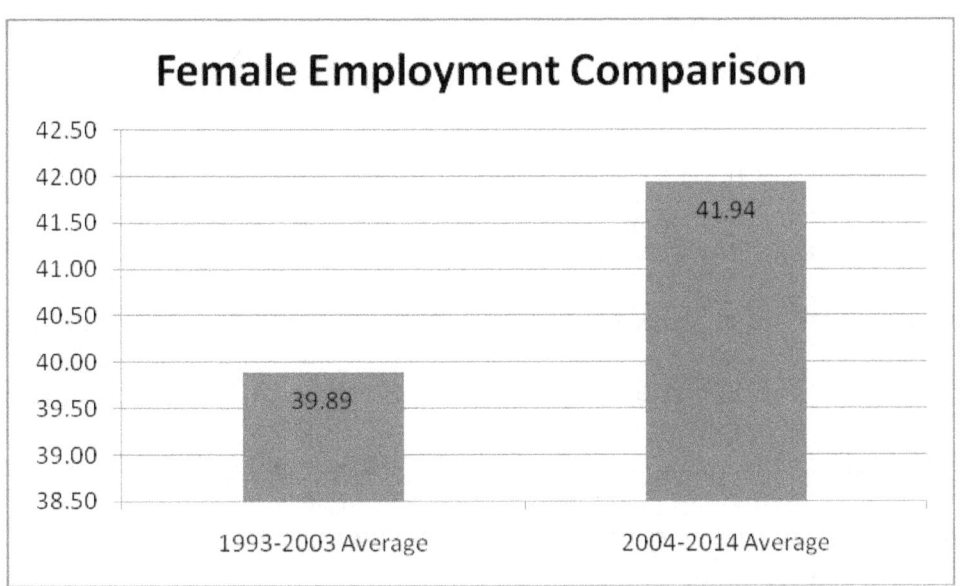

Female Employment Comparison

There was consistent reporting for female employment to population ratios by most of the 193 nations analyzed for both the 1993 to 2003 time period and the 2004 to 2014 time period to the World Bank Group. From the data obtained, it can be concluded that the annual employment to population ratio for females who were fifteen years or older increased by 5% between the 1993 to 2003 time period and the 2004 to 2014 time period. There was an annual employment to population ratio for females who were fifteen years or older positive shift of 2.05 between the 1993 to 2003 time period and the 2004 to 2014 time period. Females contribute to societies and nations in many ways, but they are often limited at the domestic level in their educational and employment opportunities (UNICEF, 2008). This lack of empowerment results in the inability to be part of decision-making processes within their families and societies, and the lack of resource allocations that results from the inability to gain education and good employment causes a cycle of being undervalued and underrepresented in societies. Females and males have different roles in societies throughout the world, but, historically and in many developing countries, females are only permitted to work within their homes. Despite working primarily in their households, many females find themselves powerless in making decision regarding household spending and healthcare, which is attributed to the lack of income and material goods that they earn and bring into a marriage. Married females tend to be younger and less educated than their husbands in developing countries, but, in situations in which females have greater influence over household decision-making, research has shown that their children survive longer, have better health, and are more likely to attend school. Females have increasingly been joining the workforce throughout the world over the last three decades, but they still do not have the same employment opportunities as males in most countries throughout the world. Females typically have less time to engage in paid work because of cultural norms that dictate that they take care of household duties and childcare. When females do gain paid employment outside of their homes, they earn 20% less than males worldwide. The paid employment that females do gain is typically informal, low paying, offers little job security, and without benefits. Throughout the world, females own fewer assets than men, and, in many countries, inheritance laws make it impossible for females to acquire assets, which leave them and their children at increased risk of poverty. Paid employment does not always benefit females because of unsafe working conditions and the negative effects it has on their children, and many females who do gain paid employment typically lack quality childcare, which often results in older siblings caring for younger ones instead of attending school.

The fifty-third through the fifty-sixth measurements calculated the annual employment to population ratio averages, percentage of change, and shift for males who were fifteen years or older between the 1993 to 2003 time period and the 2004 and 2014 time period for 193 nations in the world with the exception of Nauru and the Vatican City State (Nations Online, 2016).

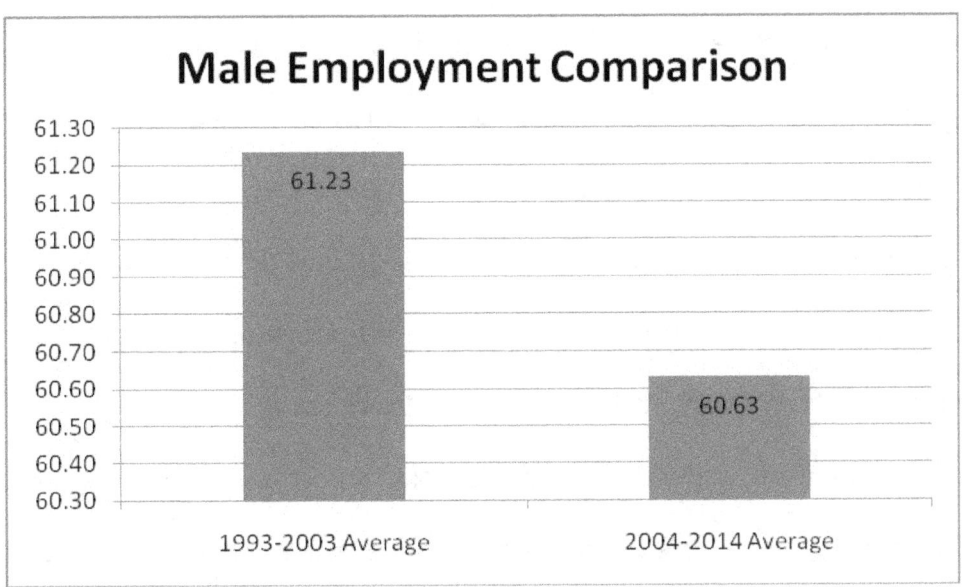

There was consistent reporting for male employment to population ratios by most of the 193 nations analyzed for both the 1993 to 2003 time period and the 2004 to 2014 time period to the World Bank Group. From the data obtained, it can be concluded that the annual employment to population ratio for males who were fifteen years or older decreased by 1% between the 1993 to 2003 time period and the 2004 to 2014 time period. There was an annual employment to population ratio for males who were fifteen years or older negative shift of .61 between the 1993 to 2003 time period and the 2004 to 2014 time period. The Global Recession in 2008 and 2009 started in developed countries, but its impact was felt around the world (International Labor Organization, 2009). Despite the financial effects of the Global Recession throughout the world, the impact of the global recession on most developing countries resulted in a slowdown of average per capita growth, but their growth has not reversed and become negative. There is also a consensus among most economists that developing economies are less effected by economic slowdowns as a result of poor distribution of wealth within them, but the Global Recession did negatively impact incomes across all countries and per capita incomes throughout the world. This deceleration in growth, however, can have a larger impact on citizens of developing nations because of inadequate social insurance systems, which has significantly impacted workers in developing countries that were previously living at or below the poverty line. Employment in most developing nations is part of a human survival strategy and does not allow the luxuries that occupations can bring in developed economies. For developing economies, the Global Recession impacted their ability to borrow from international banks, and it impacted their inflow of remittances from skilled migrant workers abroad. It also negatively impacted national capital investment by foreign organizations because of debt pressures in developed economies, and it resulted in trade contractions. These combined factors have had a systemic effect in developing economies in combination with stagnated growth in developed economies over nearly the last decade, which have resulted in decreased job growth, poorer wages, and lower living standards throughout the world.

Conclusion

In a comparison of the first through fourth measurements and the ninth through twelfth measurements, it is evident that annual primary completion rates have risen for both males and females that were twenty-five years or older between the 1993 to 2003 time period and the 2004 and 2014 time period for 193 nations in the world with the exception of Nauru and the Vatican City State (Nations Online, 2016). Male primary completion rates for those who were twenty-five years or older increased by 75% between the 1993 to 2003 time period and the 2004 and 2014 time period, and female primary completion rates for those who were twenty-five years or older increased by 78% between the 1993 to 2003 time period and the 2004 and 2014 time period.

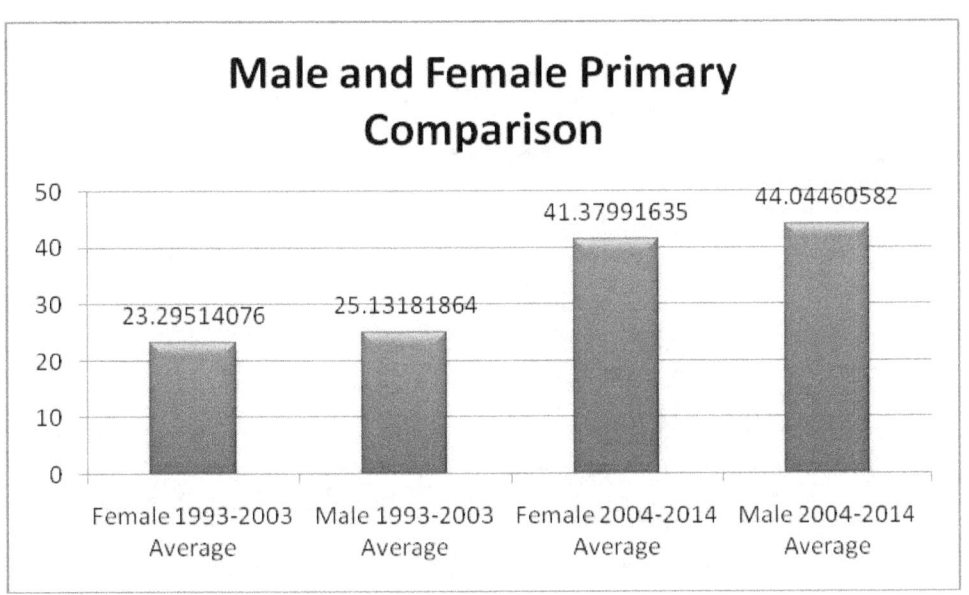

Male and Female Primary Comparison

23.29514076 — Female 1993-2003 Average
25.13181864 — Male 1993-2003 Average
41.37991635 — Female 2004-2014 Average
44.04460582 — Male 2004-2014 Average

In a comparison of the fifth through ninth measurements and the thirteenth through sixteenth measurements, it is evident that annual primary completion rates have risen for both males and females that were twenty-five years or older between the 2007 to 2010 time period and the 2011 and 2014 time period for nations that reported annual primary completion rate data every year from 2007 to 2014 for 193 nations in the world with the exception of Nauru and the Vatican City State. Male primary completion rates for those who were twenty-five years or older increased by 1.2% between the 2007 to 2010 time period and the 2011 and 2014 time period, and female primary completion rates for those who were twenty-five years or older increased by 2.1% between the 2007 to 2010 time period and the 2011 and 2014 time period.

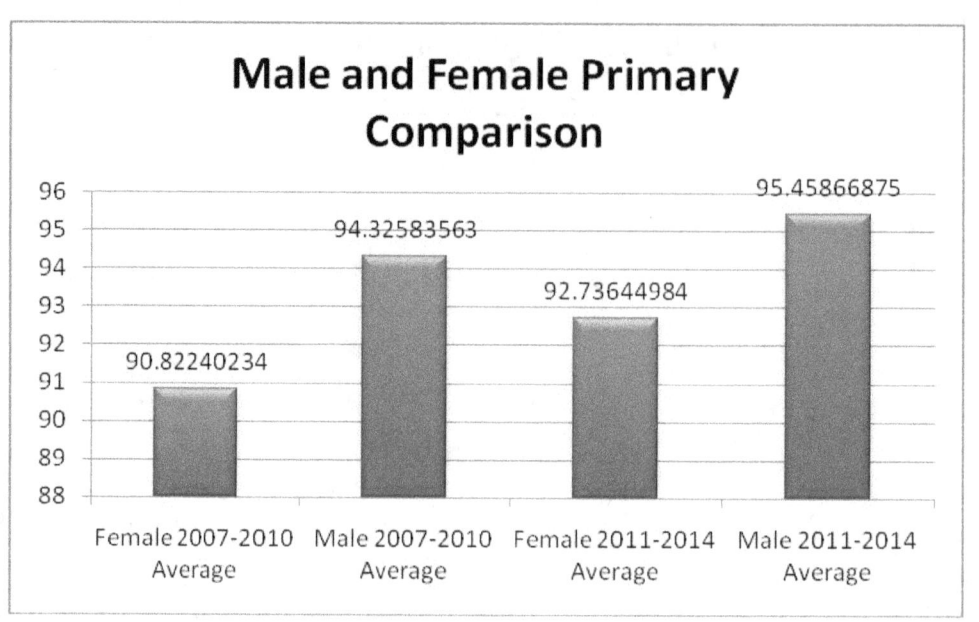

Male and Female Primary Comparison

In a comparison of the seventeenth through twentieth measurements and the twenty-fifth through twenty-eighth measurements, it is evident that annual lower secondary rates have risen for both males and females that were twenty-five years or older between the 1993 to 2003 time period and the 2004 and 2014 time period for 193 nations in the world with the exception of Nauru and the Vatican City State. Male annual lower secondary completion rates for those who were twenty-five years or older increased by 107% between the 1993 to 2003 time period and the 2004 and 2014 time period, and female annual lower secondary completion rates for those who were twenty-five years or older increased by 113% between the 1993 to 2003 time period and the 2004 and 2014 time period.

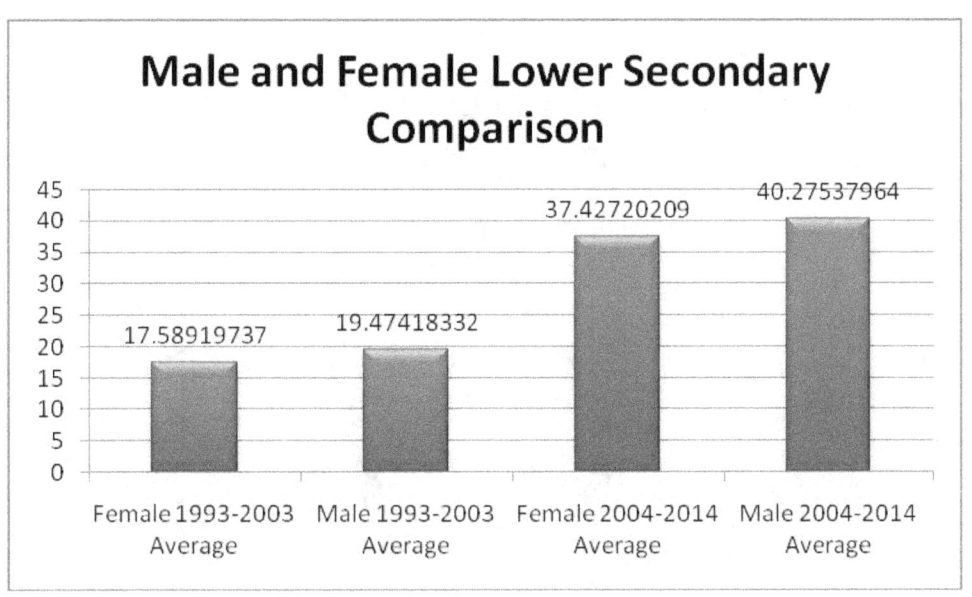

In a comparison of the twenty-first through twenty-fourth measurements and the twenty-ninth through thirty-second measurements, it is evident that annual lower secondary rates have risen for both males and females that were twenty-five years or older between the 2009 to 2011 time period and the 2012 and 2014 time period for nations that reported annual lower secondary completion rate data every year from 2009 to 2014 for 193 nations in the world with the exception of Nauru and the Vatican City State.   Male annual lower secondary completion rates for those who were twenty-five years or older increased by 2.9% between the 2009 to 2011 time period and the 2012 and 2014 time period, and female annual lower secondary completion rates for those who were twenty-five years or older increased by 3.4% between the 2009 to 2011 time period and the 2012 and 2014 time period.

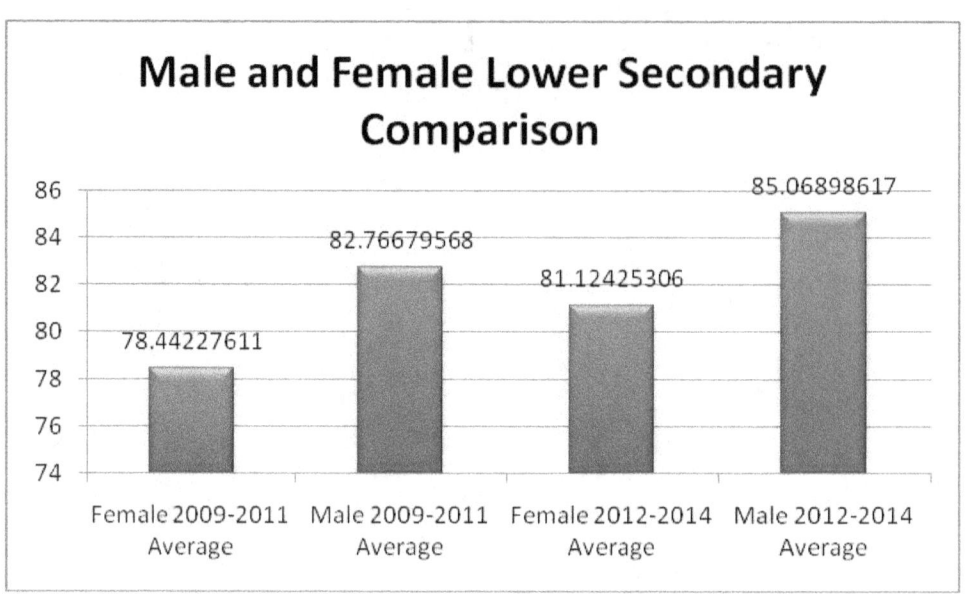

Male and Female Lower Secondary Comparison

In a comparison of the thirty-third through thirty-sixth measurements and the forty-first through forty-fourth measurements, it is evident that annual upper secondary rates have risen for both males and females that were twenty-five years or older between the 1993 to 2003 time period and the 2004 and 2014 time period for 193 nations in the world with the exception of Nauru and the Vatican City State. Male annual upper secondary completion rates for those who were twenty-five years or older increased by 126% between the 1993 to 2003 time period and the 2004 and 2014 time period, and female annual upper secondary completion rates for those who were twenty-five years or older increased by 130% between the 1993 to 2003 time period and the 2004 and 2014 time period.

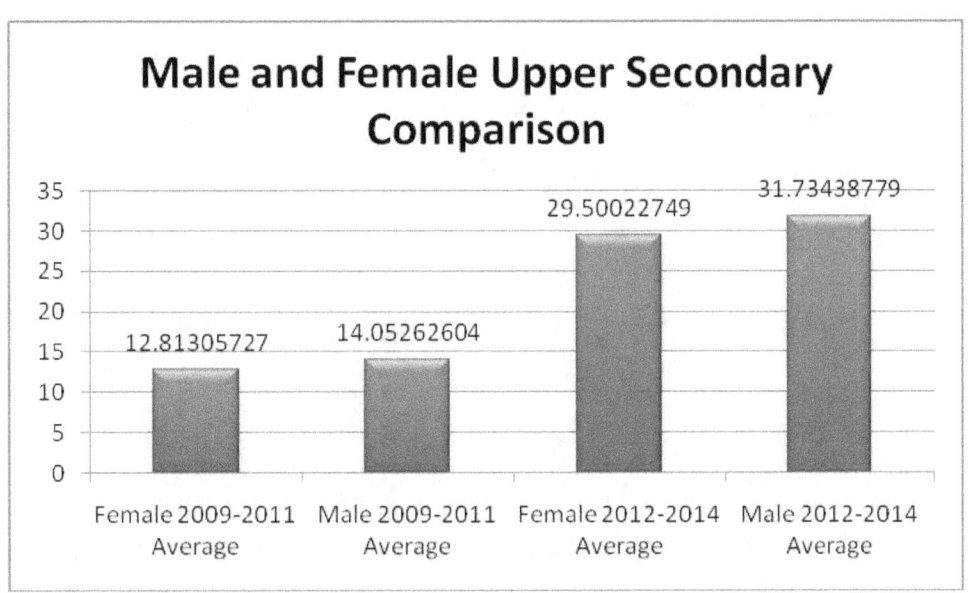

In a comparison of the thirty-seventh through fortieth measurements and the forty-fifth through forty-eighth measurements, it is evident that annual upper secondary rates have risen for both males and females that were twenty-five years or older between the 2009 to 2011 time period and the 2012 and 2014 time period for nations that reported annual upper secondary completion rate data every year from 2009 to 2014 for 193 nations in the world with the exception of Nauru and the Vatican City State. Male annual upper secondary completion rates for those who were twenty-five years or older increased by 2.6% between the 2009 to 2011 time period and the 2012 and 2014 time period, and female annual upper secondary completion rates for those who were twenty-five years or older increased by 3.3% between the 2009 to 2011 time period and the 2012 and 2014 time period.

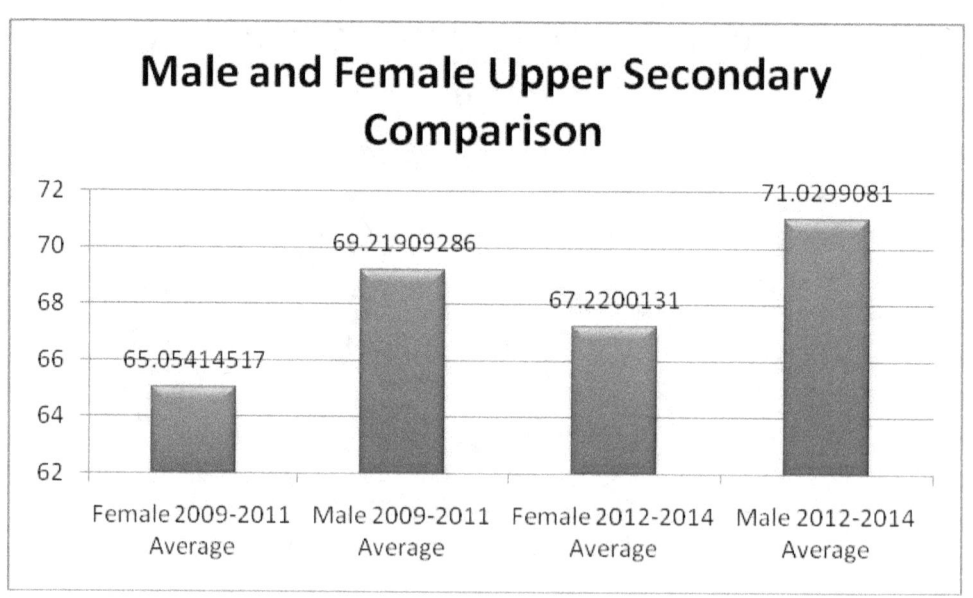

In a comparison of the forty-ninth through fifty-second measurements and the fifty-third through fifty-sixth measurements, it is evident that annual employment to population ratio has not risen for males but rose for females that were fifteen years or older between the 1993 to 2003 time period and the 2004 and 2014 time period for 193 nations in the world with the exception of Nauru and the Vatican City State. Male annual employment to population ratio for those who were fifteen years or older decreased by 1% between the 1993 to 2003 time period and the 2004 and 2014 time period, and female annual employment to population ratio for those who were fifteen years or older increased by 5% between the 1993 to 2003 time period and the 2004 and 2014 time period.

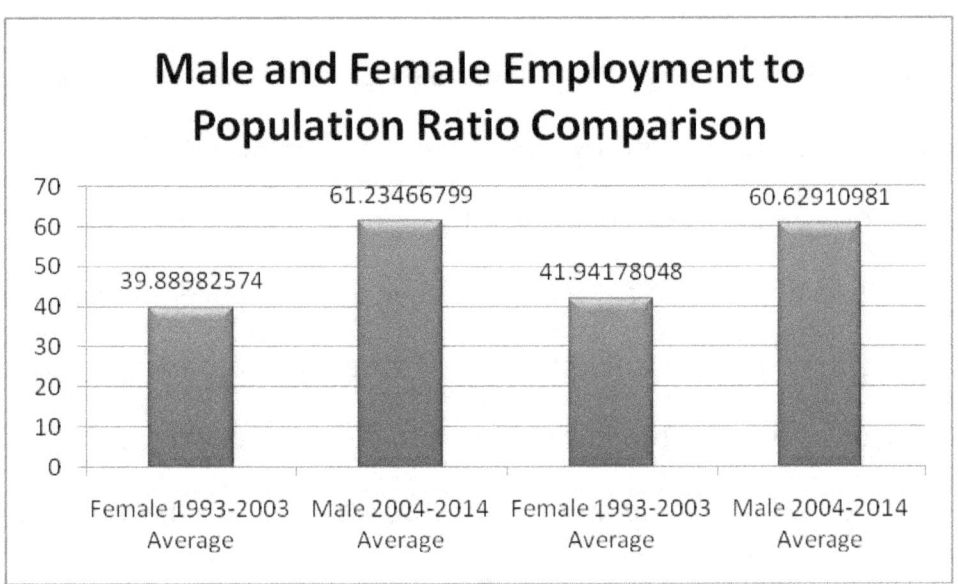

Male and Female Employment to Population Ratio Comparison

39.88982574	Female 1993-2003 Average
61.23466799	Male 2004-2014 Average
41.94178048	Female 1993-2003 Average
60.62910981	Male 2004-2014 Average

The data collected on annual primary, lower secondary, and upper secondary completion for 193 nations in the world with the exception of Nauru and the Vatican City State is positive, and it shows that more children and adolescents throughout the world are being educated. Although completion rates were lower for females for annual primary, lower secondary, and upper secondary, the data still shows that increasing numbers of female children and adolescents throughout the world are being educated at higher rates than in the past. This is positive in consideration of the gender gaps and gender biases that still exist today in both developed and developing nations throughout the world. Areas that are still of serious concern in relation to gender parity besides education are employment opportunities, political participation, and legal rights that are non-existent or biased toward females in many nations throughout the world. Education can led to empowerment only if it is supported by laws that are enforced to bring equity to all of a nation's citizens, and, despite the progress females have made in gaining education, full recognition and empowerment will not be recognized until this is rectified at the national level for females in every nation throughout the world. The data regarding the annual employment to population ratio for males showed a slight decrease employment for males, which was interesting. Although the annual employment to population ratio for males decreased by 1% between the 1993 to 2003 time period and the 2004 and 2014 time period, it is unclear why it decreased. Reasons for the annual employment to population ratio for males are beyond the scope of this study, but it is recommended that they be researched in the future in separate analyses. The data regarding the annual employment to population ratio for females showed an increase of 5% between the 1993 to 2003 time period and the 2004 and 2014 time period. This can be considered positive for females, and it shows that females' educational skills and abilities are being better utilized throughout the world. There were fewer females reported in annual employment to population ratio between 1993 to 2003 time period and the 2004 and 2014 time period in comparison to males to the World Bank, so it is clear that gender biases and gender gaps still exist in relation to utilizing female workforces throughout the world despite the progress that has been made. It is not entirely clear from the data the type of employment being engaged in by either sex, so it is likely that some of the data contains employment statistics from work that is informal, low paying, offers little job security, and without benefits. The hypothesis of the study was found to be true, and females are showing progress in relation primary, lower secondary, and upper secondary schooling throughout the world. Females are also working in greater numbers, and they are being empowered by more forms of paid employment throughout the world. Gender parity has not been reached in relation to primary, lower secondary, and upper secondary completion, and it has not been reached in relation to annual employment ratios either. Progress has clearly been made toward achieving gender parity in edcucation, poltical participation, and employment opportunities, but there are still gender gaps perpetuated by gender biases in many parts of the world today.

Reference Citations

Baughman, J. (2007). Females and Education. In *American Decades*. (Vo1. 2, p. 1910-1920). Independence, KY: Gale Cengage Learning.

Filmer, D. (2005). If You Build It, Will They Come? School Availability and School Enrolments
in 21 Poor Countries, Journal of Development Studies, 43(5), p. 901-930.

Flax, J. (2007). Gender Equality. In *The New Dictionary of the History of Ideas*. (Vol. 2, p. 701-706). Independence, KY: Gale Cengage Learning.

Grendler, P. (2006). Education. In *The Encyclopedia of the Early Modern World*. (Vol. 2, p. 232-243). Independence, KY: Gale Cengage Learning.

International Labor Organization (2009). The Global Recession and Developing Countries. Retrieved online from: http://www.ilo.org/wcmsp5/groups/public/---ed_emp/---emp_elm/---analysis/documents/publication/wcm_041819.pdf.

Nations Online (2016). A World Countries List. Retrieved online from: http://www.nationsonline.org/oneworld/countries_of_the_world.htm.

The World Bank Group (2016). Data. Retrieved online from: http://data.worldbank.org/.

The World Bank Group (2014). Gender at Work. Retrieved online from: http://www.worldbank.org/content/dam/Worldbank/documalest/Gender/GenderAtWork_web.pdf.

The World Bank Group (2008). Girls' Education in the 21st Century. Retrieved online from: http://siteresources.worldbank.org/EDUCATION/Resources/278200-1099079877269/547664-1099080014368/DID_Girls_edu.pdf.

UN Department of Public Education (2010). Achieve Universal Primary Education. Retrieved online from: http://www.un.org/millenniumgoals/pdf/MDG_FS_2_EN.pdf.

UNESCO (2015). Gender and EFA 2000-2015: Achievements and Challenges. Retrieved online from: http://unesdoc.unesco.org/images/0023/002348/234809E.pdf.

UNESCO (2011). Global Education Digest 2011. Retrieved online from: http://www.uis.unesco.org/Library/Documalests/global_education_digest_2011_en.pdf
.

UNESCO (2005). Secondary Education Reform. Retrieved online from: http://www.unesco.org/education/posit_paper.PDF.

UNESCO (2009). World Atlas of Gender Equality in Education. Retrieved online from: http://www.unesco.org/new/fileadmin/MULTIMEDIA/HQ/ED/pdf/Atlas-education-gender-equality1.pdf.

UNICEF (2008). Empowering Females: Empowering Children. Retrieved online from: https://teachunicef.org/sites/default/files/documents/units-lesson-plans/gender_equality_-_an_introduction.pdf.

UNICEF (2015). Fixing the Broken Promise of Education for All. Retrieved online from: http://www.uis.unesco.org/Education/Documalests/oosci-global-report-en.pdf.

UNICEF (2016). Globally, four out of five children of lower secondary school-age are enrolled in school. Retrieved online from: http://www.data.unicef.org/education/secondary.html.

UNICEF (2011). The State of Children 2011. Retrieved online from: http://www.unicef.org/adolescence/files/SOWC_2011_Main_Report_EN_02092011.pdf.

UNICEF (2014). Why are Boys Under-performing in Education? Retrieved online from: http://www.unicef.org/eapro/report_why_are_boys_underperforming_FINAL.pdf.

Utomo, A., Reimondos, I., McDonald, P., and Hull, T. (2014). What happens after you dropout? Transition to adulthood among early school-leavers in urban Indonesia, Demographic Research, 30(41), p. 1189-1219.

www.ingramcontent.com/pod-product-compliance
Lightning Source LLC
Chambersburg PA
CBHW052003280526
45793CB00005B/838